"ROYAL ECCENTRICS"

BY

BARBARA CARTLAND

This book required an enormous
amount of research and I am
deeply grateful for the untiring
help of Audrey Elliott, Hazel Clark,
and Sally Barnes.

Drawings by Trefor Salter.

"ROYAL ECCENTRICS"

ISBN 0 905377 44 3

First Publication in Great Britain

Copyright © 1989 Cartland Promotions

Published by
Marwain Publishing Limited
Marwain House
Clarke Road
Mount Farm
Milton Keynes
MK1 1LG

Typeset by
Grillford Limited, Granby, Milton Keynes

Printed and bound by
Richard Clay, Bungay, Suffolk

ABOUT THE AUTHOR

Barbara Cartland, the world's most famous romantic novelist, who is also an historian, playwright, lecturer, political speaker and television personality, has now written over 490 books and sold nearly 500 million copies all over the world.

She has also had many historical works published and has written four autobiographies as well as the biographies of her mother and that of her brother, Ronald Cartland, who was the first Member of Parliament to be killed in the last war. This book has a preface by Sir Winston Churchill and has just been republished with an introduction by the late Sir Arthur Bryant.

"Love at the Helm" a novel written with the help and inspiration of the late Earl Mountbatten of Burma, Great Uncle of His Royal Highness The Prince of Wales, is being sold for the Mountbatten Memorial Trust.

She has broken the world record for the last thirteen years by writing an average of twenty-three books a year. In the Guinness Book of Records she is listed as the world's top-selling author.

Miss Cartland in 1978 sang an Album of Love Songs with the Royal Philharmonic Orchestra.

In private life Barbara Cartland, who is a Dame of Grace of the Order of St. John of Jerusalem, Chairman of the St. John Council in Hertfordshire and Deputy President of the St. John Ambulance Brigade, has fought for better conditions and salaries for Midwives and Nurses.

She championed the cause for the Elderly in 1956 invoking a Government Enquiry into the "Housing Conditions of Old People".

In 1962 she had the Law of England changed so that Local Authorities had to provide camps for their own Gypsies. This has meant that since then thousands and thousands of Gypsy children have been able to go to School which they had never been able to do in the past, as their caravans were moved every twenty-four hours by the Police.

There are now fourteen camps in Hertfordshire and Barbara Cartland has her own Romany Gypsy Camp called Barbaraville by the Gypsies.

Her designs "Decorating with Love" are being sold all over the U.S.A. and the National Home Fashions League made her, in 1981, "Woman of Achievement".

Barbara Cartland's book "Getting Older, Growing Younger" has been published in Great Britain and the U.S.A. and her fifth Cookery Book, "The Romance of Food", is now being used by the House of Commons.

In 1984 she received at Kennedy Airport, America's Bishop Wright Air Industry Award for her contribution to the development of aviation. In 1931 she and two R.A.F. Officers thought of, and carried the first aeroplane-towed glider air-mail.

During the War she was Chief Lady Welfare Officer in Bedfordshire looking after 20,000 Service men and women. She thought of having a pool of Wedding Dresses at the War Office so a Service Bride could hire a gown for the day.

She bought 1,000 gowns without coupons for the A.T.S., the W.A.A.F.s and the W.R.E.N.S. In 1945 Barbara Cartland received the Certificate of Merit from Eastern Command.

In 1964 Barbara Cartland founded the National Association for Health of which she is the President, as a front for all the Health Stores and for any product made as alternative medicine.

This has now a £500,000,000 turnover a year, with one third going in export.

In January 1988 she received "La Medaille de Vermeil de la Ville de Paris", (the Gold Medal of Paris). This is the highest award to be given by the City of Paris for ACHIEVEMENT – 25 million books sold in France.

In March 1988 Barbara Cartland was asked by the Indian

Government to open their Health Resort outside Delhi. This is almost the largest Health Resort in the world.

Barbara Cartland was received with great enthusiasm by her fans, who also fêted her at a Reception in the city and she received the gift of an embossed plate from the Government.

OTHER BOOKS BY BARBARA CARTLAND

Romantic Novels, over 490 the most recently published being:

Hidden by Love	The Dangerous Marriage
Walking to Wonderland	Good or Bad
Lucky Logan Finds Love	This is Love
Born of Love	Seek the Stars
The Angel and the Rake	Escape to Love
The Queen of Hearts	Look with the Heart
The Wicked Widow	Safe in Paradise
To Scotland and Love	Love in the Ruins
Love and War	Coronation of Love
Love at the Ritz	A Duel of Jewels

The Dream and the Glory (In aid of the St. John Ambulance Brigade)

Autobiographical and Biographical:

The Isthmus Years   1919-1939
The Years of Opportunity   1939-1945
I Search for Rainbows   1945-1976
We Danced All Night   1919-1929
Ronald Cartland (With a foreword by Sir Winston Churchill)
Polly — My Wonderful Mother
I Seek the Miraculous

Historical:

Bewitching Women
The Outrageous Queen (The Story of Queen Christina of Sweden)
The Scandalous Life of King Carol
The Private Life of Charles II
The Private Life of Elizabeth, Empress of Austria
Josephine, Empress of France
Diane de Poitiers
Metternich — The Passionate Diplomat
A Year of Royal Days

Sociology:

You in the Home	Etiquette
The Fascinating Forties	The Many Facets of Love
Marriage for Moderns	Sex and the Teenager
Be Vivid, Be Vital	The Book of Charm
Love, Life and Sex	Living Together
Vitamins for Vitality	The Youth Secret
Husbands and Wives	The Magic of Honey
Men are Wonderful	The Book of Beauty and
Woman the Enigma	Health

Keep Young and Beautiful by Barbara Cartland and Elinor Glyn
Etiquette for Love and Romance
Barbara Cartland's Book of Health

Cookery:

Barbara Cartland's Health Food Cookery Book
Food for Love
Magic of Honey Cookbook
Recipes for Lovers
The Romance of Food

Editor of:

"The Common Problem" by Ronald Cartland (with a preface by the Rt. Hon. the Earl of Selborne, P.C.)

Barbara Cartland's Library of Love
                    Library of Ancient Wisdom

"Written with Love" Passionate love letters selected by Barbara Cartland

Drama:

Blood Money
French Dressing

Philosophy:

Touch the Stars

Radio Operetta:

The Rose and the Violet (Music by Mark Lubbock) Performed in 1942.

Radio Plays:

The Caged Bird: An episode in the life of Elizabeth Empress of Austria Performed in 1957.

General:

Barbara Cartland's Book of Useless Information with a Foreword by the Earl Mountbatten of Burma.
(In aid of the United World Colleges)

Love and Lovers   (Picture Book)

The Light of Love   (Prayer Book)

Barbara Cartland's Scrapbook
(In aid of the Royal Photographic Museum)

Romantic Royal Marriages

Barbara Cartland's Book of Celebrities

Getting Older, Growing Younger

Verse:

Lines on Life and Love

Music:

An Album of Love Songs sung with the Royal Philharmonic Orchestra.

Films:

The Flame is Love
A Hazard of Hearts
The Lady and The Highwayman

Cartoons:

Barbara Cartland Romances (Book of Cartoons) has recently been published in the U.S.A., Great Britain, and other parts of the world.

Children:

A Children's Pop-Up Book: "Princess to the Rescue"

Videos:

A Hazard of Hearts
The Lady and The Highwayman

CONTENTS

EMPRESS ANNA OF RUSSIA

ANNA, EMPRESS OF RUSSIA
1693-1740

Anna was thirty-seven when she ascended the throne of Russia.

She was coarse-featured and bad tempered.

Her sullenness was not altogether surprising as in 1710 she had married the Duke of Courland, who had expired on their honeymoon.

For nineteen years she lived in humiliating poverty in Courland, a dependency which passed from Russia to Prussia and then to Poland.

She existed on lean beef and pickled cabbage and wore dresses made for her by her serving woman.

A Baltic Baron wrote to a friend:

"She is a most venomous cicatrice and vulgar to boot. She has been known to count apples on a tree for fear her gardener would cheat her."

Anna soon made it plain, however, that her meanness sprang from necessity rather than parsimony.

She arrived in Moscow with a very handsome and unscrupulous lover, Ernst Biren, who was the grandson of a stable-boy.

She proceeded to lavish on him all the riches and honours at her command.

She built him a Palace in St. Petersburg, and gave him estates in Courland, Livonia, Silesia and the Ukraine, making him the greatest landowner in Russia.

Biren had a passion for horses and Anna constructed a Riding-School for him which became the meeting place for Society.

She then created a Department of State to care for Biren's mares and stallions.

The Austrian Minister, Ostein wrote:

"When Monsieur de Biren speaks of horses he talks like a man, but when he speaks of men, he talks like a horse."

In fact, Biren's pleasure was to terrorize men.

He had however no desire for political power and left affairs of State in the hands of the Vice-Chancellor.

He liked to be recognised as the first man of the Empire, and he was not happy unless Princesses of the blood and Ministers were trembling before him.

He soon found a method of ensuring servility.

He set up an inquisitorial department, known as the Secret Chancellery. Soon the country was honeycombed with spies and informers.

Anyone who dared to criticise the new regime soon found himself in the torture chamber.

Biren singled out for persecution the old Moscow nobility who had opposed the candidature of Anna.

Some were broken on the wheel, some impaled, others thrown into dungeons or banished to the Arctic.

It is said that some twenty-thousand Russians were exiled, a quarter of whom disappeared without trace.

The great Russian Historian, Kluchevsky wrote:

"The issues of life or death depended on his smile or his frown. If he were pleased to be merry, everyone was boisterous with mirth; but if he raised his voice in anger his crowded ante-chamber emptied itself in a minute."

Biren was well aware of the growing enmity and persuaded the Empress to have 'her person guarded by retainers from Matau and other Courland localities.'

This caused German officials to accumulate in Moscow 'like chaff sprinkled from a leaky sack,' so that they overran the Court, besieged the throne, and grabbed every administrative post to which any sort of salary was attached.

This increased the hatred of foreigners and accelerated the horrible activities of the Secret Chancellery.

But to the Empress Biren was irresistible and she could not refuse any of his demands.

She made him her Grand Chamberlain, and a Count of the Empire.

Later, she bribed the Courlanders into electing him their reigning Duke with the title of 'Most Serene Highness' and the right to sit with reigning Princes.

Biren's passion for luxury inspired Anna to try and create the most elegant Court Russia had ever known.

St. Petersburg at that time was a muddy City of wooden houses.

The Empress ordered the Winter Palace to be partly rebuilt and she designed for her servants an elaborate green livery laced with gold.

She then announced that everyone was to equip his house with carpets, mirrors and pictures.

She ordered a dressing-table for herself with a mirror made of solid gold.

People gossiped about 'baths of white wine,' an easing stool of silver studded with sapphires, toothbrushes with handles embellished with rubies.

The first Ball held in the new Gallery of the Winter Palace created a sensation.

Lady Rondeau, wife of the British Minister wrote:

"Though it was very cold the stoves kept it warm enough, and it was decorated with orange-trees, and myrtle in full bloom; these were ranged in rows that formed a walk on each side of the hall, and only left room for dancers in the middle. The walks on each side gave the company an opportunity to sit down sometimes, as they were hidden from the presence of the Sovereign. The beauty, fragrance and warmth of this new formed grove, when you saw nothing but ice and snow through the windows, looked like enchantment. . . ."

Russia was heading for ruin because of a combination of bad harvests and declining commerce.

The Empress however refused to curtail her extravagance.

The British Minister wrote to Lord Harrington:

"Your Excellency cannot imagine how magnificent this Court is since the present reign although there is not a

13

shilling in the Treasury and nobody is paid."

Despite the poverty, the Empress frowned on anyone who wore the same costume twice to her Balls and masquerades.

As a suit cost anywhere from £150 to £200 many of the Foreign Ministers wrote home asking for increased allowances.

Rondeau wrote:

"I never saw such heaps of gold and silver lace laid upon cloth. I cannot imagine that this magnificence will last many years, for if it should, it must ruin most part of the Russian nobility, for several families are obliged to sell their estates to buy fine clothes."

However, despite the Empress's extravagance her Court was not very elegant.

Foreign Diplomats described her preference for sky-blue or apple-green garments, and for ugly handkerchiefs tied round her head which all her ladies were obliged to copy.

No one, they reported, was well groomed.

Fine materials were badly tailored, rich dresses crumpled and stained, smart uniforms topped by incongruous wigs.

Expensive carriages were drawn by wretched half-dead animals.

The wife of the British Minister was one of the few people who did not find the Empress repulsive to look at.

Although she refers to 'an awfulness in her countenance that strikes you at first sight', she continues:

". . . but when she speaks she has a smile about her mouth that is inexpressibly sweet. . . ."

Yet that mouth could harden into a cruel line, for Anna had a taste for sadism.

"She knew how to mingle barbarism with extravagance so crudely as to make foreign observers absolutely gasp with amazement." wrote Kluchevsky.

Like Peter the Great Empress Anna had a craze for dwarfs and jesters, and anyone who displeased her was compelled to serve in a position of degrading buffoonery.

Elderly men were forced to become her pages and fetch and carry like boys.

Others who fell out of favour, men and women alike, were made to ape the antics of animals for the general amusement of the Court.

When a member of one of the great Boyar families called Nikita Volkonsky annoyed her, he was made to sit in a specially constructed basket and to cackle like a hen for hours at a time.

The distinguished General, Apraksin, who made the mistake of marrying a Roman Catholic, had to go on all fours and bray like a donkey.

Prince Michael Golitsyn also married a Roman Catholic and committed the further error of embracing that same religion.

The Empress commanded him to become her page, but this was only the start of his punishment.

She had just completed building an elaborate Ice Palace at a cost of £7,000 when Golitsyn's wife died.

She ordered the unfortunate widower to marry again and chose his bride herself: a servant girl called Anna Buzheninova, who was considered the ugliest girl in all Russia.

When the Prince saw her face, which apparently resembled that of a Pekingese dog with a skin problem he knew the Courtiers had not been exaggerating.

There were a procession of Anna's collection of deformed and freakish human beings to lead the wedding party.

Then, in carriages pulled by pigs, dogs and goats came the worst of the drunken reprobates in St. Petersburg.

They were followed in mock pomp by representatives of Russia's component States in their national dress.

The bridal pair travelled to Church in a cage on the back of an elephant.

After the ceremony a Reception took place in Biren's Riding-School where the bride and bridegroom were forced to sit on a dais watching the merry-making.

The couple were then taken to the Ice Palace beside the deeply frozen River Neva.

The Palace was 80 ft. long, 32 ft. high, 23 ft. deep and every part of it was made of blocks of ice which had been meticulously measured.

Carved completely of ice was a vestibule, a Ball-room and a bed-room with the four-poster, mattress, quilt and pillows also of ice.

The year was 1740, it was during the depths of winter and here Golitsyn and his bride had been ordered to spend their wedding night.

The jeering crowd forcibly bedded them down for the night and guards were posted by the sealed ice doors.

Miraculously the couple survived their Arctic honeymoon even though they had been stripped naked.

After that the Empress lost interest in them and instead reverted to her interest in shooting.

She kept loaded guns by the windows so that she could take pot shots at passing birds.

Nine months after his unforgettable night in the Ice Palace Golitsyn's ugly little wife presented him with twin baby boys.

It was reported later that their sons lived long and happy lives.

Money was growing shorter and shorter and Biren ordered his minions to seize goods and chattels from the poverty-stricken population.

The wars fought during Anna's reign were costly farces.

One was fought for the Polish succession, in which the French emerged the sole victors.

Another was against the Turks in the Crimea, the result of which was to recapture Azov at the cost of thousands of dead Russians.

The smouldering hatred towards 'the German party' began to solidify, and the minds of many people turned to the daughter of Peter the Great, Elizabeth, as the only possible saviour.

Ever since the Empress Anna's succession, Elizabeth had been living quietly in a country house near Moscow.

Biren would not allow her to hold Court, nor encourage her to visit St. Petersburg more than once or twice a year.

Elizabeth was only twenty-one, and was quite happy to be left alone.

She liked outdoor sports, riding, hunting and skating.

In November, 1740, the Empress was seized with a fit at the dinner table and was taken to bed unconscious.

It was obvious that she was dying and Biren begged her to name him as Regent.

Besotted though she was, Anna knew that Biren was hated too much to last as Ruler for long.

"Duke, Duke", she cried, "my heart is sad for you, for you are encompassing your own ruin!"

She then turned her face to the wall and died.

The four-months-old Ivan VI was now Emperor of Russia.

Biren survived as Regent for no more than three weeks, when he was arrested in the middle of the night by Field Marshal Munnich and sent to the Arctic.

ROSHANA AND BOBBY

THE MAHARAJAH OF JUNAGADH

The Maharajah of Junagadh, Sir Mahabat Khan Babi Pathan, is the only man known to have a large wedding for two of his dogs.

He decided to cross his favourite bitch Roshana with a golden retriever call Bobby.

He also decided that if they were going to mate they should be married first, and he ordered a dog wedding to take place, in the most spectacular manner.

It was a full blown State occasion and there were 50,000 guests. The Viceroy was sent an invitation but declined.

A huge procession of elephants was organised and a guard of honour for the Bride.

She was perfumed and covered in jewels, and the Bridegroom wore gold bracelets on his legs, with a cummerbund of silk embroidered with jewels around his middle.

There was a formal banquet after the ceremony with Bobby and his wife seated on the Maharajah's right, this giving them precedence over all the Royalty present.

When the Banquet was finished the happy couple were taken to the Bridal suite where the union was consummated.

Bobby then returned to the kennels, but Roshana, being pregnant, spent the rest of her life on velvet cushions in her bedroom.

The Indian Maharajah had such a liking for dogs that he kept an enormous number of them and spent a huge percentage of his State's income on maintaining them in splendour.

His pack at one time numbered over 800 and his most favoured dogs each had his own room with electric light and a telephone.

They all had their own personal servant who attended to their every wish.

If a dog was ill with distemper or any other complaint

there was a hospital consisting of three white tiled wards supervised by an English Vetinerary Surgeon.

Naturally this excellent attention meant that the hospital lost very few patients.

A few of course, died and they were then laid in a lined casket with a Band playing Chopin's Funeral March to accompany the cortege.

The Maharajah spent large sums in buying up Crufts' Champions every year.

The cost of running this Paradise cost £2,300 a month which was actually 11 percent of the State's revenue.

The pedigree dogs gave him many hours of intense study before he decided who would mate with whom.

There was no doubt that the Maharajah's children envied the dogs who came first in their father's affections.

But the Maharajah was also a sadist. He enjoyed watching hounds which had been deliberately starved killing and fighting over a crippled antelope.

As the days of the Raj were numbered the new Government of India wondered what the Maharajah's reactions would be to the political crisis.

Rumours reached Delhi that Pakistan had promised him troops and money.

Besides however, the political consequences Junagadh's defection gave them concern for the sacred River Saraswati watered the State and the relics of an ancient Hindu culture and two Holy mountains made it a place of pilgrimage.

There was also a granite boulder on which the immortal Asoka had chiselled fourteen edicts.

Junagadh was also the last refuge in India for the lion.

Its hills encompassed the Gir Forest which was five hundred miles of thorn scrub that blazed scarlet in the Spring with blossoms of the flame of the forest.

The Princes of Junagadh invited Nobility to shoot two or three of the lions, but they did protect them on the whole so that today some three hundred survive much to the annoyance of the local farmers because they often leap on the bullocks.

While Sir Mahabat Khan hesitated, the Indian Government surrounded Junagadh with infantry, tanks and sent a squadron of fighters.

The Maharajah's only artillery was two sixteenth century bronze cannon of Persian make.

He therefore decided it would be a mistake to order his Lancers to defend him.

With all his jewellery, four of his dogs, and three of his four wives, he boarded his private plane to take up residence in Pakistan.

The fourth wife followed him the next day when she found her child she had somewhat absent-mindedly mislaid.

H.M. KING FAROUK OF EGYPT

H.M. KING FAROUK OF EGYPT
1920-1965

Farouk, Prince Said, the last King and the last Pharoah of Egypt, was born on the 11th February 1920, two weeks prematurely.

Upon his arrival King Fuad gave the doctor who delivered the Prince 1,000 in gold, ordered 10,000 to be distributed to the poor and 800 pounds to the Mosques. One hundred and one guns fired a salute to the young Prince.

The first person who looked after Farouk was an English midwife named Lucy Sergeant. Then he was passed on to a village girl from Govcala in Turkey, who breast-fed him.

He was a voracious feeder, and this must have established his appetite, for he was a glutton for the rest of his life.

He was a good baby, seldom cried, and he shared his childhood with his parents and four sisters.

His main home was an enormous stone Palace at Adbin, which had 550 rooms.

His Mother was Queen Nazli, younger than her husband by thirty years. King Fuad had divorced his former wife to marry Nazli, the daughter of a noble Franco-Egyptian family.

Together with the midwife, and his governess Ina Naylor, Queen Nazli ruled Farouk's young life.

But being the only boy amongst four sisters, there was a bitter rivalry between Naylor and the Queen for Farouk's affection.

He had an elder sister from King Fuad's first marriage, called Fewkia, who was twenty years older than he was.

The other girls were Fawzia, Faiza, Faika and Fathia.

King Fuad thought the letter 'F' brought luck to the family, and Farouk, when he grew up, also chose names with an 'F' for his children.

Farouk played in the Palace in the Byzantine Room, in

the Suez Canal Room, and crawled under Louis XVI beds.

In the summertime everyone went to the beaches of Alexandria, and to the Tas el Tin and Montazah Palaces. In the cooler season from October to March they were in the Abdin and Kubba Palaces.

All the Palaces were lavish, and had magnificent grounds, with beds of glorious flowers, with pools and streams.

King Fuad built his son a schoolhouse in the grounds of Montazah Palace, beside the sea, where the Prince could still carry on his studies.

As a child he was fairly fit, but suffered with a weak chest, poor eyesight, and abscesses in his ears.

He was brought up by women and surrounded by them, so he became the darling of the Queen and her Ladies-in-Waiting, who spoiled him continuously.

Queen Nazli enjoyed the occult and went every night to a woman in the Palace to hear incantations over a smoking cauldron, taking Farouk with her.

This affected him and he was soon unable to sleep before 3 a.m. in the morning. So his relatives hit on a way to keep him amused by teaching him to gamble.

The King also put his son on a diet to try to keep him slim, but the Prince was so hungry one day, that he had to eat the cat's dinner.

The Prince's principal hobbies were photography and fishing, together with motoring. He had his first car at the age of 12, an Austin Seven, and his second car was given to him at the age of 15, which was a present from his father.

By 1936 the King's health deteriorated rapidly and on the night of 27th April, it was obvious he was dying.

He eventually died on Wednesday 29th, and nine hours later Farouk was proclaimed King of Egypt.

When he became King at the age of 16, he wanted to race his cars without any restrictions.

Early in his reign the local Police stopped him when he was going too fast, and to avoid this happening again he had all his cars — over one hundred of them — painted fire-engine red.

He also made it illegal for anyone else to own a car of that colour.

After that he could speed as fast as he wanted.

If any other motorist tried to pass him he would shoot at their tyres.

On Thursday 29th July 1937, King Farouk I of Egypt and the Sudan ascended to the throne.

At this time the City of Cairo was a spectacle.

Two million people arrived and for three days the population was tripled. Tons of mutton and beef were roasted and given out in the streets, and there were illuminations everywhere.

King Farouk was seventeen when he drove his Alfa Romeo to Alexandria to ask Safinaz Zulficar to be his wife. She agreed, although she was only fifteen.

The King remembered his father's example, and changed her name to "Farida" meaning "The Only One."

The date for their Wedding was set for 20th January 1938.

The Wedding was mostly a Moslem affair, although Farida did break with tradition by watching the Ceremony through a grille, and by posing for her photographs without a veil.

They received amazing presents, from a Sevres Porcelain Dinner Service, to a tray of pure gold.

Cairo again looked like a fairground, and once more meat was carved and cooked in the streets.

Queen Nazli had chosen Farida for her son, because she thought she would be submissive.

But Farouk fell in love with Farida, and she was anything but subservient. She became a Queen equal to Nazli herself, and they soon came into conflict.

On the 17th November 1938, forty-one guns fired a salute to announce a daughter had been born to Queen Farida. Seven days of celebrations followed, and there were free food and clothes for the poor.

During the first three years of his marriage King Farouk gave his wife a present every single morning. They ranged from priceless jewels and furs, to Paris dresses and object d'art.

Queen Farida's influence over her husband was very strong, and she put an end to his domination by his mother.

There were terrible scenes in the Palace and King Farouk would go out into the desert to avoid his wife and mother.

He had a desire to purchase anything that he fancied whether it was any use to him or not.

He started to steal things that belonged to other people. To make sure that he could do it well, he had a prisoner taken from the Tural Jail to teach him the rudiments of pick-pocketing.

He practised being proficient at this by wearing a suit to which tiny bells had been sewn, and in time he became so skilled that he could take anything without the bells ringing, and anyone being aware of it.

At parties and receptions he would brush against the Dignitaries and their Ladies, and later when they were over, he would empty his pockets of watches, wallets, powder compacts and lighters.

He even took Winston Churchill's pocket-watch from his waistcoat and only under pressure did he agree to return it.

After a few years he had a whole warehouse filled with the things he had purloined.

These even included the Ceremonial Sword, belt and medals which he had stolen from the body of the Shah of Persia, as it passed in State through Egypt in 1944.

Farouk organised looting parties to the houses left by German residents who had fled from Cairo at the start of the War.

He stripped their homes of everything that remained.

He also thought out a very clever scheme known as "Farouk's Treasure Box".

One of his staff would get in touch with a Business-man with the suggestion that the King would appreciate the gift of a box of chocolates.

The man would then go to Ahmed Naguib's shop, which was the place suggested and discover that although the chocolates were cheap, the box was very expensive.

It was in fact, a jewel encrusted casket and cost £650.

Because he thought it would be wise to please the King the business-man would pay the sum, and present the casket to Farouk.

He immediately ate the chocolates, returned the box to the shop and in doing so transfered £650 into his own pocket.

He thought out a number of other fiddles which always paid him handsomely.

In 1942 during the War, King Farouk was given the ultimatum by the British either to appoint Nahas Pasha as Prime Minister, or to Abdicate.

He appointed Pasha but this affected the King greatly. Always unstable and nervy, he became prey to psychological tendencies.

He felt persecuted and lived his life at night, and slept during the day. He also became fat and aged prematurely.

On his birthday 11th February 1942, there were enormous crowds in the Square in front of the Abdin Palace. The King was most touched and sent a message to his people thanking them.

During the week of parties following his birthday the King met Princess Fatima Toussaun and fell madly in love with her. He drove past her house in the hope of seeing her.

He went as far as declaring he wanted to divorce Queen Farida, but was persuaded not to do so.

In November the King was travelling along a road to Ismailia when a British truck came in the opposite direction, forcing him off the road.

"I am the King of Egypt," he said to the soldier who came up to him.

"And I am The Emperor of Afghanistan," replied the English voice.

King Farouk in some ways never grew up, and behaved just like a naughty boy. He kept a car horn which, when sounded, was like the howl of a dog being run over. He liked to sound this when it would make the most impact.

Another time at a Country Reception, he put an ice cube down the bra of a lady guest to "help her to keep cool!"

When lions featured in a number of his nightmares, he was so bothered that he went to Cairo Zoo one morning, and shot every single one of the beasts in their cages.

In his Palace at Abdin he could lay 600 places with gold plate for dinner, and he had a private Theatre which could seat 400, where he had shows and films.

By the time King Farouk had reached the age of twenty-five, his appearance had changed enormously.

He was over six feet tall, very fat, with bags under his eyes.

He used to wear a moustache which was waxed at the ends like his father.

He loved to surprise friends, and would arrive at a Villa in shorts, grey socks and gym shoes, looking for someone to go swimming with him.

Even at a formal dinner he would throw pellets at guests, an act of extreme childishness. When he hit the person he was aiming for, he would laugh hysterically.

One night, after Queen Farida had moved out of the Palace taking with her three daughters, King Farouk was returning home with a girl-friend when he was stopped and as he was unrecognised he was robbed.

Then they were both stripped and left. They returned to Cairo and the King telephoned his Valet to bring him some clothes.

When he returned to the Palace, he put on a uniform and went to the prison which held the captured robbers and asked for the one who had suggested shooting him to step forward.

When the man did so the King shot him.

After the War ended King Farouk went away each summer to Cyprus. In his villa he kept a suitcase full of money for gambling.

He went out in dark glasses with a Gardenia or a Carnation in his buttonhole, and would throw wild parties with Greek girls dancing round a fire. The parties were late and licentious.

Purple Hearts kept in his shaving cabinet gave him a lift, and he smoked hashish.

He would spread his bed with newspaper and let his pet rabbit play on it, and other rabbits were brought in to mate with it.

He loved these times when he could relax, and would do so for five months of the year, consuming large meals, with caviare being specially flown in for him.

He enjoyed being with his servants, his parrot, his rabbit and the girls!

After five years of marriage, his sister Fawzie returned to Egypt to get better after a bout of Malaria. She did not return to the Shah of Persia.

When Fawzia unpacked her bags Farouk grabbed the Persian Crown Jewels she had with her for his collection.

In November 1948 King Farouk and Queen Farida were divorced, and the King lost the remaining respect of his countrymen by this act.

He continued to eat enormously and consumed vast quantities of liquid. He even had to have special chairs built for him.

When darkness came Farouk became a different person, and went out to the Nightclubs.

The weeks of the King's life as a Playboy continued with whole floors of hotels being taken over and thousands of pounds being expended on the turn of a card.

The King was warned that the patience of the people would not last for ever.

On the 11th February Farouk announced his engagement

to Narriman Sadek. She was sixteen, he was thirty. On the 6th May 1950 they were married.

Farouk grabbed all the gold wedding presents which they had been given, and melted them down into gold bricks, and they were packed away in the hold of his luxurious pleasure yacht.

He and his wife honeymooned on the Isle of Capri, booking all the 150 rooms in the Hotel.

His honeymoon lasted thirteen weeks and cost £1,000 a day.

On one year just before his birthday, a decree was sent out that he would accept only gold presents, and when they arrived they were all melted down and flown in a private plane to secret Banks in Switzerland.

Someone once heard Farouk say:

"I am now as rich as the Nizam of Hyderabad!"

In 1952 Crown Prince Ahmed Fuad was born to Queen Narriman, a month premature, and the birth was announced by the King himself.

But it was too late. The public could not forgive him.

It was not surprising that he was extremely unpopular and in 1952 was deposed by Colonel Nasser.

It was when Egypt's new Government went through what the King had left behind that they were astounded.

The Palace was exactly like 'Aladdin's Cave' and the treasure he had collected took months even to catalogue.

There were innumerable strange objects from his pick-pocketing mixed with obscene novellettes, pictures and magazines from his pornography collection.

In one were discovered eight hundred and fifty thousand coins and medals in gold, one hundred and sixty-four in platinum. One thousand two hundred and sixty-one works of art in gold and silver.

There were hundreds of valuable clocks and watches and four drawers filled with gold fountain pens and diamond studded dice.

He had every type of luxury article Georgian scent

flagons, enamelled or gold knives, gold patch boxes, and a great series of snuff boxes.

There was a great variety of watches, gold and silver, French and English. Some in the form of shells, flowers and butterflies. Watches made in London and Geneva. The list was endless.

When Sotheby's staff arrived to catalogue the objets d'art they found the Guards using a Faberge Imperial Easter Egg as a football.

The soldiers guarding the collection had used the automatic erotica so much that they were exhausted.

The majority of the silver was of Egyptian, Turkish, French and English origin, and Farouk had collected about five hundred paperweights, including some very rare ones.

Just before the Auctioneer started, a Representative for the Egyptian Government stood up and said that anyone who bid £5,000 or over, would be granted access to the pornographic collection. This was a great incentive for a lot of people.

The Auction went on for weeks, and raised over seven hundred thousand pounds.

Farouk had settled for the moment in a Villa near Rome. He was now thirty-two years of age but weighed nearly twenty stone.

He raced his cars, went to Night-clubs with his body-guards and ate enormous meals.

In 1954 the Ex. Queen divorced him and her place was taken by a succession of prostitutes.

His women however much he gave them, did not cost as much as his gambling.

He lost twenty-five thousand pounds one night at Deauville Casino and five million francs at baccarat in just a few hours.

His losses began to reach one million a year and Farouk had to reduce his staff to twelve and cut his enormous number of cars down to three and a small yacht.

When he was forty he spent most days in a darkened

room eating chocolates, drinking fruit juices and watching television.

In Exile in Italy Farouk was much quieter and could be seen driving a maroon Mercedes occasionally.

One night at a Nightclub he met Irma Capece Minutolo, who thereafter stayed with him for years.

His health deteriorated and he became an old man very quickly, living just for his many children.

He would rather pathetically telephone old friends just to see how they were getting on.

He never failed to write to the midwife Lucy Sergeant, and he remembered birthdays and Christmas but was rather forgetful in his conversation, and would tell the same stories over and over again.

In March 1965 he left a Heart Clinic in Switzerland, and Sonia Romanoff visited him, and listened whilst he relived the old days in Egypt.

On the 17th March he visited Irma Capece at her flat, and sat listening to television.

He rose from the chair rather heavily, and left to drive to the house of Annamaria Gatti, whom he had arranged to see that night.

He collected her and they drove to a roadside Inn called *'Ile de France'*.

At midnight they started a dinner of one dozen oysters, Lobster Thermador, three portions of Roast Lamb, chips and string beans, and enormous helping of chestnut trifle and two oranges.

Farouk lit a Havana cigar when suddenly it fell from his hand, and his head fell back.

He was driven to the hospital of San Camillo while several doctors tried to do what they could for him.

Ten minutes later at 2.08 on the 18th March 1965, at the age of forty-five Farouk was dead.

One prophecy that he made remains amongst his sayings:

"Soon there will only be five Kings left," he told Ex-King Zog of Albania. "Spades, Hearts, Diamonds, Clubs and the King of England."

PRINCESS SHAN-YIN OF CHINA
b 456

Princess Shan-Yin of China was very much in advance of her age.

She was born in 456 A.D. and her brother Ts'am Wu came to the throne in 473 when she was seventeen.

After he was fully established as Ruler she complained to him that while he had over three thousand concubines with which to enjoy himself, she had only one lover.

The King who was very fond of his sister agreed that it seemed somewhat unfair and the next day he sent to her thirty young men, one for every day of the Chinese month.

The Princess was very grateful and delighted.

She made out a time-table for the men and insisted that they did not break the rules but kept her amused for months.

After a little while however, she thought it over and decided it was really rather boring having only one young man at a time.

So she ordered an enormous bed, the largest ever made and when it was done the boys joined her in it and she spent unusually exciting nights among them all.

PRINCESS SHAN-YIN OF CHINA

PETER THE GREAT
1696-1725

Peter the Great was the first Tzar ever to leave his own country and in 1697 he toured Western Europe.

He wore sailor's clothes and hobnobbed with ordinary workmen and his manners stunned society.

He did not know how to use a table napkin; he belched, broke wind, and picked his teeth.

He had such an alarming temper that people were afraid to meet him.

One observer marvelled that 'the Providence of God . . . had raised up such a furious man to so absolute an authority over so great a part of the world.'

The Electress of Hanover, a granddaughter of James I of England, found Tzar Peter 'charming'.

She said he was very gay, very talkative and 'we established a great friendship'.

But with all the advantages with which nature had endowed him, it could be wished that his manners were a little less 'rustic'.

She went on:

'He told us that he worked himself in building ships, showed us his hands, and made us touch the callous places that had been caused by work.'

He mistook the whalebones of ladies' corsets for the real thing and showed his astonishment by saying that the German ladies had 'devilish hard bones.'

People often commented on the convulsions of his face and limbs and he at times turned his eyes so that one could see nothing but the whites.

Peter journeyed with a retinue of 250 people known as the Great Embassy.

Françcois Lefort was one of Peter's closest friends, a Swiss adventurer who drank 'like a hero' and had been given the title Governor-General.

At banquets Peter made Lefort sit at the head of the

table and frequently startled Western Diplomatists by standing in servant's dress behind Lefort's chair.

The Royal entourage consisted mainly of lackeys, guards, musicians and Court dwarfs.

It also included twenty nobles and thirty-five young men chosen by the Sovereign and known as 'Volunteers'.

After six months in Holland the Tzar went to London.

King William III of England presented him with a gift of a private yacht, *The Transport Royal,* which was armed with twenty brass cannon.

The Tzar crossed the North Sea in this vessel, moved into a barge on the Thames, and was rowed past the Tower, under London Bridge and lodged in a house in Norfolk Street.

Three days later King William called on him and was received by Peter in his shirt-sleeves.

King William was said to have nearly fainted from the foulness of the air in his room and was appalled to find that the Tzar was sleeping with four other people in one small room, the windows of which were tightly closed.

Peter toured the usual sights and found an actress, Miss Cross, who became his mistress; and much of the night was given to wild parties.

The curtains were slashed and carpets ripped, pictures were used for target practice, and the great holly hedge was ruined because of the Tzar's enthusiasm for a wheelbarrow which he had never seen before.

He drove it backwards and forwards through the shrubbery.

The Tzar's travels came to an abrupt halt in the middle of 1698 soon after his arrival in Austria.

He received a message that in Russia the obstreperous *Streltsy* musketeers were rebelling once again.

Peter hurried home, but the revolt was over by the time he reached Moscow.

Several hundred *Streltsy* musketeers had been executed and seventeen hundred imprisoned in Monasteries.

He learned that the main cause for the rebellion was the fact that hundreds of musketeers had been dragged from their families to go and fight in the Azov area.

The pay was bad, the food inedible and the punishments excessive.

Needless to say, Peter was not satisfied. He had heard that it was rumoured he was dead and Sophia was to take his place.

He was determined to uncover what he was sure was a deep-laid plot against him.

He now behaved so diabolically that the events of 1682 paled into insignificance.

He had fourteen torture chambers set up on his private estate, each one in the charge of a sadistic subordinate.

The seventeen hundred *Streltsy* musketeers imprisoned in the Monasteries were sent to Preobrazhensky to be slowly roasted alive.

Thirty furnaces were lit each day while Peter watched the process with relish ordering doctors to revive those who fainted.

After torture came the executions and finding the headsmen too slow, Peter picked up the axe himself and sent his subjects' heads rolling in the dust.

He stood, a Royal giant with contorted features foam-flecked lips and clothes stained with his victims' blood.

He had the bodies dangling from gibbets which were erected at every gate leading into the Capital.

Even the Musketeers' wives were tortured and killed.

The massacre continued for six months, ending in February, 1669 when 195 Musketeers were hanged, some holding in their lifeless hands a copy of the petition in which they begged for mercy.

No one was allowed to be buried until the Spring.

The sight of their fleshless skulls impaled on iron spikes made it clear to the people of Moscow what was waiting for them if they rebelled again.

Peter's favourite amusements were Burlesques of

appalling coarseness.

Christmastide, Twelfth Night and the Carnival before Lent were celebrated each year with fantastic rites.

Peter and his nobles roamed the streets dressed as patriarchs and Bishops followed by a 'Drunken Synod' composed of the most dissolute men in Moscow.

On other occasions he forced the dignitaries of the City to don ridiculous costumes and ride in carts drawn by cows, goats, dogs and pigs.

Matthew Golovin, a man of illustrious family, who was eighty years old, was ordered to take part in one of these processions dressed as a devil.

He refused and Peter ordered him to be stripped naked. A cap with horns were forced onto his head and he was made to sit on the frozen Neva for an hour.

He caught pneumonia and died a few days later.

The diabolical Theodore Romodanovsky who was known as the King of Pressburg and addressed by Peter as 'Majesty' was dressed up in silks and satins.

Sometimes the mock Tzar was dressed like the Biblical David, in bear-skins and carrying a lyre.

Everything about Peter's Court was crude and coarse.

He delighted in making his guests partake of things they most hated, whether it was eating oysters which made them ill, dressing in ludicrous clothes, or drinking until they collapsed to the floor unconscious.

A great bumper of brandy, drunk without a pause, was the worst experience that could befall a Courtier.

At every orgy a number of unfortunate people were singled out for this ordeal, which frequently proved fatal.

A Danish Minister described an occasion when he knelt before the Tzar and asked to be let off with one and a half pots of wine instead of the regulation couple.

Peter roared with laughter and forced him to swallow half a dozen bumpers while he knelt so that by the time he was allowed to stand up he could not keep on his feet.

On the way home from these banquets he reported seeing the ice-bound river and snow-covered fields 'black with the bodies of drunken men and women, sleeping it off under the open sky, like the slain on a battlefield.'

Many of them never rose again because they were frozen to death during the night.

Apart from revelling in drunkenness, Peter took a delight in making his guests physically sick.

One of the original Trustees of the British Museum wrote from Moscow:

"The Russian cooks often tie eight or ten mice on a string and hide them under green peas, or in such soups as the Russians have the greatest appetite to, which sets them kicking and vomiting in a most beastly manner, when they come to the bottom and discover the trick; they often bake cats, wolves, ravens and the like, in their pastries and when the company have eaten them up, they tell them what they have in their guts."

He attacked the Dutch Minister with his fists, and the Duke of Holstein's Minister with the flat of his sword.

He frequently sent other men reeling across the room.

What he enjoyed more than anything else was to see his guests fighting each other.

For this reason he always invited two or three hundred people for dinner, but only provided seating for a hundred.

The company sat down without any Grace, crowded so closely together that they had difficulty in lifting their hands to their mouths.

Carpenters and shipwrights sat next to the Tzar, but Senators, Ministers, Generals, Priests, sailors, buffoons of all kind, sit pellmell, without any distinction.

If Peter's Court was fantastic, so was his personal life.

He had sexual relations with his favourite Alexander Menshikov; he married a servant girl and made her Empress, and he murdered his son and heir, Alexis.

Peter visited Europe again and was hospitably entertained in France, where he made a favourable impression on his hosts.

Praise froze to horror however when they heard the

stories that filtered out of Russia about the appalling treatment of his son and heir Alexis.

Alexis was the son of Eudoxia: a frail, intelligent, sensitive dreamer in his late twenties.

Unlike his father, he was happier with a rosary in his hand than a sword.

It infuriated Peter to have what he called a 'physical weakling' for a son.

He tried desperately to mould the boy in his own image.

He sent him to war as a bombardier, into the docks to build ships, to sea on a galley.

He forced him to study engineering and mathematics.

Alexis was so frightened of his father that he often fainted when summoned to his presence.

Once, when Peter asked to see a mathematics paper he had set him, he shot himself in the hand to provide an excuse for not completing it.

Peter forced Alexis to marry a German Princess, Sophia Charlotte of Blankenburg-Wolfenbuttel, to whom luckily he became deeply attached.

However the Tzar kept the bride so short of money that she lived in abject poverty.

After four years of misery she gave birth to a son, Peter, and promptly died.

Alexis was beside himself with grief, but he received a heartless letter from his father on the day of the funeral, furious with him for not giving 'any attention to military affairs.'

He threatened:

"Be quite sure that if you do not change your attitude I will cut you off as though you were a gangrenous swelling."

Alexis wanted nothing more than to be free of his terrible father.

He wrote back renouncing the succession on grounds of ill-health.

This so enraged Peter that he wrote a second letter

offering his son a chance of 'mending his ways' or becoming a Monk.

Without a moment's hesitation, Alexis chose the Monastery and signed his reply:

"Your slave and useless son, Alexis."

At the end of August Peter sent him a further letter telling him that if he wished to remain his heir he must join him at the battlefront without delay.

Alexis escaped to Vienna accompanied by a pretty Finnish girl, Afrosina, with whom he was now deeply in love.

He was hysterical with fear that his father might pursue him, and asked the Austrian Emperor to grant him political asylum.

Tzar Peter was furious, regarding the flight of the Tzarevich to a foreign potentate as nothing less than treason.

He instructed his ablest Diplomat, Count Peter Tolstoy to get Alexis back at any cost, and in order to make the task easier he handed him an autographed letter for Alexis in which he swore 'before God and His judgement seat' that if he returned to Russia he would not be punished but 'cherished like a son.'

This done, he went off on his Western tour with Catherine.

It took Tolstoy eighteen months to make Alexis do as his father wished.

Every pressure was put on the terrified young man, including threats against his beloved Afrosina.

However, a second letter from the Tzar assured him that he would be allowed to marry Afrosina and live quietly on his estates.

Peter arrived back in Russia at about the same time as Alexis.

What happened next can only be compared to the punishment of the *Streltsy*.

Peter was determined to uncover the plot.

Alexis was subjected to days and weeks of interrogation, sometimes by his father, sometimes by Tolstoy.

It was clear that Alexis had never lifted a finger to either depose Peter or to secure the succession.

It was clear, however, that a large number of people looked upon Alexis as their only hope.

'The Clergy, Nobility, the common people,' the Hanoverian Resident Webber, reported to his Government, *'respect the Tzarevich like a God.'*

The Clergy regarded Peter as an anti-Christ, the Nobility as a man who had sold Russia's soul to foreigners.

Whatever they felt, Alexis had done nothing treasonable, and when he was confronted by his awful father his will collapsed and he was persuaded that every mark of sympathy shown towards him, every chance encounter, every stray remark, had been a crime.

He supplied a list of his friends, who subsequently were tortured and killed.

Kikin, the man who had advised him to go to Vienna was broken on the wheel.

Finally, poor Afrosina was brought before the inquisitors.

Under threat of punishment, she incriminated Alexis by repeating all his confidences.

She revealed that he hated his father, longed for his death, rejoiced when he learned of plots against him, and had pledged himself to restore Moscow as the Capital.

Peter went mad with fury.

He sentenced Alexis to twenty-five strokes of the knout.

This terrible instrument was a whip made of parchment and hardened in milk so that it could cut to the bone with every lash.

Probably Alexis was not intended to survive the punishment, as five days later he was given another fifteen lashes, but still he did not die.

Peter decided to take no more chances.

That night he convened the High Court, composed of

his own hand-picked creatures, and asked them to decide Alexis's fate.

Without any need of discussion the 127 members condemned the Tzarevich to death 'for having desired the death of the Sovereign, plotted the ruin of his country, of his lord and father, with the aid of foreign arms.'

As Peter had given an oath to respect the life of Alexis he could not bring himself to sign the sentence.

Instead, the Tzarevich was confined in the Trubetskoy bastion.

In the Day Book of the Guard an item appears on 26th June stating that in the presence of the Tzar and others torture was applied.

Another sentence records that on the same day in the evening, Alexis Petrovich died.

Peter issued an Imperial rescript describing his demise as 'an act of God.'

Few people accepted it.

It was generally believed that Alexis had been killed by a sword or an axe, and the Dutch Resident reported that his veins had been opened.

No one knows the truth; only that Peter visited the prison on his son's last day.

Tzar Peter gave a banquet and a Ball the following night.

When Peter was fifty-three years of age, although his energy still appeared to be inexhaustible, he looked an old man.

At the end of January 1725 he was forced to take to his bed, suffering from a stone in the kidney.

He ran a fever and at times was in such pain that he screamed in agony and tore the bed-clothes.

His mind turned to his successor and he asked for some paper with which to write, but he only wrote two words: *'Give all,'* and the pen dropped from his hands.

He called for his daughter, Anna, to dictate his Will, but when she arrived a few minutes later he could not speak.

For sixteen hours, with palsied face and bloodshot, staring eyes, the giant Tzar lay breathing out his life.

The Priests never ceased to pray.

He died on the 8th February, 1725 and Catherine closed his eyes.

PETER THE GREAT

H.M. KING PHERON OF EGYPT

H.M. KING PHERON OF EGYPT

Pheron was King of Egypt and the successor of Sesostris became blind because he was bold enough to throw a dart on to the waters of the River Nile.

He was standing high above the fields where it was very windy. The King threw his dart and lost his sight.

He was blind for ten years, after which time he was told by an Oracle that the time had nearly come for his blindness to end.

If he wanted to recover his sight he was to bathe his eyes in the urine of a woman, who had only been faithful to her husband, and had never slept with any other man.

He began to use the urine from his wife, but that did not work.

He obtained some from other women, and at last was successful, and he regained his sight.

He then ordered that all the women whose urine had not helped him were to be taken to a town where they were to be burned alive, together with the whole occupants of the town.

He then married the woman whose urine had cured his blindness, and was so thankful that he built two obelisks in the Temple of the Sun.

Alas, his wife did not prove to be so chaste after marriage.

Furious, the King asked her why she had remained faithful to her first husband.

Whereupon she replied:

"No other man ever asked me before!"

TZAR IVAN THE TERRIBLE

THE FIRST TZAR – IVAN THE TERRIBLE
1530-1581

Ivan the Terrible was born on 25th August in 1530, during a raging thunderstorm and this seemed to set the pattern of his life.

He suffered a depressed childhood and by the time he was eight years old he was an orphan. He was kept short of both food and clothing and even his fostermother was taken from him.

He was brought up by men who had no idea how to do it. Violence in every form took place right in front of him and soon became a part of his feelings and imagination.

He grew older in an atmosphere of continual battle, giving back blow for blow.

His earliest enjoyment shared with friends was hideous. He watched as men were tortured.

He saw men tantalising beasts until he was able to do so himself, and one of his great amusements was derived from throwing dogs from the top of the Castle and watching their agonies as they hit the ground.

By the time he was 14 years old Ivan was so violent that he seized power from his guardians and he had 30 of the Councillors hung on gibbets by the roadside.

If anyone protested at what Ivan wanted they were either imprisoned, beheaded or thrown to the dogs. If they were insolent their tongues were cut out.

In his teens, Ivan began to rampage through the streets hitting men he was near and violating women. He was applauded enthusiastically by his friends.

Ivan called his peers about him and announced he was going to be crowned not as a Grand Duke, but as Tzar.

The Coronation took place on 16th January 1547. There were peals of bells and everyone prayed the new Tzar would be granted the light of justice and truth. Handfuls of gold pieces were scattered before him.

Ivan then decided he was going to get married. All Noble

girls of marriageable age were ordered to go to Moscow and about 1,500 of them arrived.

They were housed in one building containing many rooms, each with twelve beds in it.

While Ivan looked at them through a screen so that he could not be seen, they were examined by a Doctor and a midwife.

Gradually they were discarded for one reason or another until finally there were only ten, and at last Anastasia Zakharine Koshkine was chosen.

They were married on the 3rd February 1547, and it was amazing that Ivan grew to love Anastasia.

She managed to quieten him a little and together with his mentor, a monk called Sylvester, they made his rages decrease.

His conquests made him a hero with his people.

He also became rather pious and ordered that St. Basil's Church in Moscow be built, but he had the Architect's eyes taken out, so that they could never again design anything more beautiful.

Everyone hoped that Anastasia would dispel some of the fire and anger in the Tzar, but they soon realised that this was impossible.

In 1560 Anastasia died and Ivan became tyrannical again. He smashed all his furniture and would not see his children.

His old nature had returned.

Once when the people of Pskov came to complain against their Governor, the Tzar gave them a terrible reception. Returning to the ways of his boyhood, he poured lighted brandy over them and would have had them stripped and probably put to death, had not something diverted him.

When this happened in the village of Ostrovka, a messenger came to say there was a fire in the Kremlin.

The great bell had fallen down, and it was taken as an evil omen.

Ivan carried round with him a long pointed staff and he used it to lash out at anyone who displeased him.

He would scream orders at his attendants. He would set bears on people, and would have them put under icy water if they were disrespectful.

He had peasant women stripped and used as targets for his marksmen. One day he poured some boiling soup over his Jester, and when he screamed at the pain, Ivan stabbed him to death.

He had a most peculiar sense of humour.

At a large Moscow Festival, some English and Dutch women laughed at him because of his fierce appearance.

He was furious and ordered them to be taken to his Palace, where they were stripped, led into a large hall, and servants threw on the ground 45 bushels of peas.

The women were ordered to pick them up one by one, with Ivan watching them. When the task was completed, they were all given wine and told to behave themselves in future.

On another occasion he ordered the inhabitants of a City to bring to him a cart full of live fleas.

This they were unable to do. They could not capture and keep the insects, because they were scratching themselves, having all been infested with fleas all over their bodies.

Ivan roared with laughter when he heard, and fined them 7,000 roubles for not doing as he had ordered.

If he was bored, the Tzar would go down to the dungeons of Alexanorov and watch the prisoners being tortured.

Once he let it be known that he was going to a Castle in Livonia. The inhabitants were terrified when they learnt of his intentions. They decided to blow themselves up rather than face Ivan.

The Tzar took a second wife in 1561 called Maria, but she died in 1569. That year he chose another girl, but she was so terrified when she heard of his intention that she collapsed and died from the shock.

Ivan learnt that the City of Novgood was planning a rebellion, so he set out to quell it.

On the way he went through the City of Tver and burnt it to the ground, killing the people in case they were planning the same.

When he finally arrived at Novgood he built a wall of wood round the City so that no-one could get out.

Then standing on a high point he watched as 1,000 people a day were taken out and executed.

As this was taking a long time he ordered mass drownings in the Volkov river. Men, women and children were tied on to sleighs and dragged into the freezing water. If they climbed out they were pushed back in.

Eventually Ivan grew fed up with these killings and moved on leaving 50,000 dead behind him.

Ivan was such a restless man that he had to have 3 blind men telling him stories when he went to bed to help him get to sleep.

But his temper was always evident and in 1581 he argued violently with his son Ivan.

This time the Tzar went crazy and raised his iron pointed staff and and crashed it down on his son's temple. His son fell to the floor and died five days later.

The Tzar's health began to cause great concern.

His body swelled enormously and gave off an incredibly unpleasant odour.

One night he sent for a friend to play Chess with him, and as the pieces were set up, he felt faint.

Moments later the first of the Tzars Ivan the Terrible, the most horrifying tyrant, was dead.

H.M. KING STANISLAUS I OF POLAND
1677 – 1766

Deposed by his people in 1709 after a reign of only five years, they found him too expensive as he was not only a *bon viveur* but had a taste for all the good things in life regardless of cost.

Free from any responsibility he devoted the remainder of the 57 years of his life to living in a very stylish fashion.

He settled in Lorraine and collected an enormous staff to see to his comforts.

It consisted of no fewer than 510 servants and included were sixteen gentlemen of the bedchamber, four private secretaries, twelve personal valets, over forty footmen, thirty-one porters, ten Masters of the King's Horse, forty-one gardeners and sixty-three musicians.

The King's own personal staff included architects because he was particularly fond of fine buildings, in fact, this and rich food were his two great passions.

With the architects who numbered seventeen he rebuilt the city of Nancy in the Italian style.

Nobody locally was asked if this was what they wanted and one old man was so outraged at Stanislaus's 'vandalism' that he walled up his windows rather than look at the offensive new buildings.

The King's thoughts were seldom away from his stomach and the staff he hired to make sure he had what he wanted were his special joy.

They consisted of twenty-four cooks, four confectioners, seven table-deckers, five cellar and pantrymen and seven men whose job was to look after the roasts.

All of them were presided over by eight stewards, and three *maîtres d'hotel*.

Ex-King Stanislaus fermented his own version of Tokay wine and invented a number of new dishes one being sugared vegetables.

His special recipe required the bird to be plucked alive

and then whipped to death before it was cooked.

As this was one of his favourite dishes it appeared to some people only fair that at the age of eighty-nine his nightshirt caught alight.

Trying to beat out the flames he hit himself so hard that he fell unconscious into the fire and was roasted.

H.M. KING STANISLAUS I OF POLAND

PRINCE CHRISTIAN OF
SCHLESWIG—HOLSTEIN

PRINCE CHRISTIAN OF SCHLESWIG—HOLSTEIN
1831 – 1917

Prince Christian of Schleswig-Holstein was the husband of Princess Helena, and the son-in-law of Queen Victoria.

During a pheasant shoot at Sandringham, his brother-in-law the Duke of Connaught, aimed at a low flying bird — which was bad sportsmanship — missed and hit Prince Christian instead.

This meant that for ever afterwards the Prince would have to wear a glass eye.

Queen Victoria was furious and said when she heard of the accident:

"My dislike and fear of shooting will only increase!"

Prince Christian who was extremely poor, — his Mother-in-Law had often said that she gave him everything he possessed — had to make the best of what was undoubtedly a very bad job.

Despite the expense he was not content with just one glass eye, but ordered the whole range of different coloured eyes, including a blood-shot one for when he had a cold.

He had these arranged on a special tray and would make his daily selection according to how he was feeling and what he was wearing.

In fact, as the years passed he became so fond of his false eyes that he frequently showed them off at the dinner table, much to the surprise and discomfort of the other guests.

If Prince Christian asked a lady to admire the specially set out tray that was bad enough, but he often sent a servant for it in the middle of a dinner party.

Prince Christian then forced his fellow diners to watch him changing eyes.

It was in fact, something which sensitive people found ruined their appetites.

大清國慈禧皇太后

TZ'U-HSI THE DOWAGER EMPRESS OF CHINA

TZ'U-HSI THE DOWAGER EMPRESS OF CHINA
1835 – 1908

On the lovely Mountain of Ten Thousand Years, which rose above the K'un Ming Lake, there grew flowering shrubs and trees so typical of China.

Flights of marble stairs and tunnels carved in the rock led up the hill.

It was here that Tz'u-hsi — the Dragon Empress — as she was called, would go to look at the view while eating sweetmeats.

Tz'u-hsi was always accompanied by ladies and eunuchs who obeyed her implicitly.

By a mixture of indulgence and tyranny she ruled her household.

Walking beside her was the Chief Eunuch, a tall, sagging man, 'very ugly . . . his face covered in wrinkles, but he had beautiful manners.'

The Empress's Ladies-in-Waiting and her eunuchs were the immediate victims of her crotchety temper.

She dominated them by sudden outbursts of rage, then taking them aside in turn to talk to them in a conspiratorial manner, and pretending affection and concern.

In her pearl-laden high-soled shoes Tz'u-hsi was indefatigable.

She would trail her attendants along, dart into the muddy reeds at the side of the lake, and trudge through the watered beds of chrysanthemums.

One of her special joys however was the rain.

"It takes away all the defects and washes the landscape in soft mystery," she said.

But while she indulged her pleasure in real life watercolour under a huge umbrella, her eunuchs and ladies stood by miserably, soaked to the skin.

"It was a characteristic," one of them said, "that Her Majesty should experience a keen sense of enjoyment at the troubles of other people."

The Empress, who had started life as a concubine, spent £650,000,000 a year.

She ordered luncheon at any moment and in any place that took her fancy and the Eunuchs set up their stoves and cooked it.

Or sometimes they produced it from thermos lacquer containers and reheated it.

Luncheon and dinner always consisted of the same one hundred dishes from which the Empress picked and chose her favourites.

As these remained constant, the cooks pocketed a good part of the *table d'hôte* allowance by serving up day after day the same dishes she never sampled until the weevils were crawling in them visibly.

As the Empress sat at her table alone, the dishes spread before her, she sometimes favoured a lady-in-Waiting with a dainty morsel which manners forced her to eat wreathed in smiles.

As Tz'u-hsi never offered one of her special delights, the morsel was quite possibly ten days old, and she was well aware of it.

She enjoyed ordering punishments, both petty and severe.

She once made two of her maids slap each other's faces harder and harder in front of her.

Her attention to detail was tyrannical.

On one occasion she order a Eunuch called Chao to carry two special dishes, as a mark of her esteem, to Li Lienying.

Because it was raining heavy he sent one of his subordinates to do it.

When Chao reported Li Lienying's thanks to the Empress she demanded:

"Did you deliver them yourself?"

Chao said he had.

"It is raining outside," she said crisply, "so how is it your clothes are dry?"

At Chao's confusion, she sentenced him to ten strokes

of the bamboo, and she laughed as she did so.

Emperor Hsien-feng died in 1861 and it was then that Tz'u-hsi began plotting to gain the throne.

His wife, Niuhuru, who was named after the Clan to which she belonged, expected that her baby son would eventually become the Emperor of China.

It was thought, however, that the Emperor's brothers should act as Regents.

Then Tung Yuan chun, a Censor, suggested that the Dowager Empress and Niuhuru should reign together.

This suited the Dragon Empress because she knew that as Niuhuru was easily persuaded, she could seize her chance later.

Rivalry had increased between the two women over the Emperor Kuang-hsu's affections, for the child showed signs, as T'ung-chih had done, of preferring the indulgent Niuhuru to his forceful and ambitious adoptive mother.

T'zu-hsi, failing bitterly once more to win the love of a boy, became impatient with him, and although he was good at his books, unlike her own son, she so terrified the thin and unhealthy Kuang-hsu by her exhortations that he threw himself into the arms of his Tutor Weng T'ung-ho whenever she approached, as if 'facing lions and tigers'.

Jealousy between the two women may also have been stoked by memories of their mutual husband, for the popular story that quickly circulated the Capital and spread through China until it was accepted as gospel in the south was that Niuhuru, gossiping about the old days with Tz'u-hsi, revealed that Hsien-feng had entrusted her with a document.

In it the Emperor ordered that if she gave any trouble, Tz'u-hsi was to be instantly decapitated.

Niuhuru fetched the decree to show Tz'u-hsi and laughing at the changed times, tore it up before her.

That very afternoon, a Eunuch presented Niuhuru, as she gazed into a goldfish pool in the garden of the Forbidden City, with some milk cakes as a gift from

Tz'u-hsi.

Niuhuru took a mouthful. By the evening she was dead.

The Empress once said:

"Do you know I have often thought that I am the cleverest woman who ever lived and that others cannot compare with me."

However, her reactionary attitudes and her adherence to an obsolete doctrine of a Sino-centric world precipitated China into poverty, Civil War, foreign invasions, and brought about the fall of the Ch'ing Dynasty.

Her personal fortune was put at £22 million in gold and silver bullion.

Turning her face towards the South and straightening her limbs, Empress Tz'u-hsi died on the 15th November 1908.

KING PEDRO I OF PORTUGAL
1320-1369

King Pedro I of Portugal had particularly bad luck where his love life was concerned.

When he was Prince, he was betrothed to Joan the daughter of Edward III but she was struck down by The Black Death when she was on her way to marry him.

His next love was Constance of Castile who became his wife but she died five years after their wedding in 1345.

The Prince then fell in love with Inez de Castro who became his mistress and he found for a short while true happiness.

The one dark cloud hanging over them was the Prince's father King Alfonso XI.

He was the veteran of many family feuds and a dictator in every sense of the word.

When his son Pedro announced that he intended to marry Inez because they were so happy the King refused to entertain the idea.

"She may be noble," he shouted, "but no son of mine is going to marry a girl who was born illegitimate!"

Prince Pedro however, who was used to his father's rages and shouts was determined not to have his happiness ruined on what was to him a quite unimportant point.

He obtained a special dispensation from the Pope, and married Inez in secret at Braganza on New Year's Day 1355.

During the next few months Pedro and his wife were exceedingly happy.

But King Alfonso began to suspect he had been hoodwinked and it infuriated him. He was not accustomed to having anyone disobey him and he swore on every possible oath that he would be damned if he was going to tolerate it.

Pedro was out hunting when King Alfonzo faced Inez and forced her to admit that she was now his daughter-in-Law.

She apologised and begged for mercy but the old man was determined to show her none.

As soon as he had left her Villa at Quinta das Lagrinas three courtiers broke into the house and assassinated Inez and her three children.

When Pedro returned home he went nearly mad with grief and fury.

He confronted his father with the murders but the King pretended to be angry and banished the guilty courtiers from the Palace.

No-one however was fooled by the King's behaviour and Pedro vowed that when he came to the throne he would extract revenge on those who had murdered his wife and never forgive his father.

Then two years later King Alfonso died and Pedro became King.

He ascended the throne in 1357 and his first act was to order the extradition of his wife's assailants.

Only two could be found after a long hunt for them, and they were brought back from Spain, tortured in the presence of the new King and finally had their hearts torn out from their bodies.

Two years later King Pedro ordered the body of his beloved wife Inez to be exhumed from its resting place in the Cathedral at Coimbra.

He had her taken to Alcobaca. Here she was dressed in Royal Robes, anointed, placed on a throne and solemnly crowned.

Pedro sat beside his Queen and the nobility of Portugal stepped forward one by one, and lifted her dead hand and gave her their loyalty with a kiss.

When the ceremony was over the King had the newly crowned Queen sealed in a marble sarcophagus which was placed opposite one that was ready for him when he died.

Queen Inez remained there until 1810 when Napoleon's invading troops forced open her tomb in search of

QUEEN INEZ

souvenirs.

Strangely enough they also cut her hair which was still yellow, from her skeleton.

The King's wife had therefore been dug up twice, once to be crowned and once to have her hair cut.

Fortunately she has not been disturbed since and has been allowed to rest in peace.

EMPEROR NERO
37-68 A.D.

Nero was born in A.D. 37 and was the son of Agrippina, Caligula's sister, and was therefore his nephew.

He became Emperor on the death of Claudius, in A.D. 54, when he was seventeen years old.

His intellectual ability was extremely limited, but he was keen on the arts, taking part in singing, dancing, sculpture and poetry.

In the first five years of his reign he took very little interest in either domestic or foreign affairs, leaving it all to his Ministers, and thus the Senate had more liberty and they reduced the burdens on the people.

Nero set out to enjoy himself.

At night, he would put on a peasant's cap, a false beard, old garments, and would go out with a crowd of his friends, pleasure seeking and brawling.

The trophies of these expeditions, torn clothes from women, jugs and bottles from public houses, shop signs that had been torn off, or broken nozzles from fountains were taken back to the Palace, and there were either given away or auctioned.

Nero got great excitement, as did his Uncle Caligula, from enciting people to violence, and would have the guards taken away from theatres and circuses so that the opposing sides could come to blows.

These excursions only stopped when he was so beaten up by a Senator for showing insolence to his wife, that Nero nearly died.

As he got older his mother, Agrippina realised that the hold she had over him when he was small, was slipping.

So she told Nero on a number of occasions that he was on the throne only because of her, and if he did not submit to her command, she would give the throne to Britannicus, his half-brother.

This upset Nero, and it was no surprise when one night

at dinner Britannicus had what was thought to be an epileptic fit, and fell from the table, foaming at the mouth, and bruising himself on the floor. He was taken out, and eventually died.

When he was carried to the funeral pyre his bruises quickly gave rise to the rumours that Nero had poisoned him, and the purple colouring was the evidence.

Unfortunately after the death of Britannicus the relationship the Emperor had with his mother grew worse and when he could stand it no longer, he had her removed from his Palace and she was taken to live in the home of Antonia, her Grandmother.

Most of her servants were taken away from her, and very few people were allowed to see her, as they had done when she was in favour.

At twenty-one years of age Nero had the world at his feet, but all he wanted was Poppaea Sabina, a beautiful woman already married to Otho.

Nero never really cared for the wife he already had by the name of Octavia, who had been forced upon him for reasons of State.

When he was eighteen his eyes had roved to a young Greek girl by the name of Acte, but this match met with great disapproval and opposition from his mother.

Now when Nero saw Poppaea he wanted her, but as his mother still had a slight hold over him and his conduct he could not deliberately oppose her.

So he went out of his way not to see her alone, knowing that she could not reprimand him in public.

Poppaea by this time, although married, was more than willing to divorce her husband to become Empress. The idea appealed to her but the only person who stood in her way was Agrippina.

Nero personally planned his mother's death, and when her Villa was to have some repairs done to it, the posts of her four-poster bed were sawn nearly through. But she was warned of the danger by a slave, and escaped.

Nero was furious and went nearly mad that he had failed.

When one day he was attending a theatrical performance a ship appeared on the stage, and it had suddenly opened, spilling out a number of wild beasts, then closed again.

Nero grinned. This gave him the idea that he might kill his mother by similar means, and Anicetus took on the task saying that a vessel that would spill Agrippina into the sea, was easily made.

Nero decided he must be friendly to his mother, to make her less suspicious of his evil thoughts, and he tried to mend the rift between them. He wrote to her in cheerful, affectionate letters, allaying her fears.

At the beginning of March Nero went to Baiae to attend the Festival of Minerva, which was to begin on the 19th and would last for five days.

He invited his mother to join him, and when she arrived, her son descended from his ship and greeted her warmly. He presented her with a splendid new galley, all gilded and with silken sails.

Before he left his mother, he invited her to a banquet to take place the same evening, to honour her arrival. Agrippina accepted.

She was on the point of returning to her Villa, to rest and get ready for the banquet, when she was told that her own ship had been run into by another ship out in the bay.

She hesitated, then decided to travel by land rather than in the new galley, which would take a little time to prepare for her arrival.

She attended the banquet, and enjoyed herself thoroughly, with her son being most agreeable to her.

She rose to leave at about midnight, intending to return to her home by litter, the way she had arrived, but was told that the new Galley was now ready for her.

Nero bade her farewell, pretending to be very tender to her and the Galley carried her away on a warm, dark, still night.

Suddenly a signal rang through the night and the roof of her cabin which had been reinforced, caved in. A slave who was standing near Agrippina, was killed instantly.

Her maid fell into the water, screaming loudly:

"Save me! Save me! I am the Emperor's Mother!"

Thinking she was Agrippina, she was at once struck viciously by the conspirators with marlinspikes and was killed.

Agrippina was more crafty. She just slipped silently into the water, and although she was injured, she escaped by swimming away from the scene.

She was rescued by a couple of fishing boats, and she ordered them to take her to her Villa on the shore of the lake.

When the news came to Nero that his mother was still alive, he screamed, ranted and raved. But he was also terrified of what revenge she would take on him.

He was therefore extremely surprised when she ignored his part in the plot, and pretended to marvel at having been so fortunate as to escape such a bad accident.

Anicetus told Nero that he would finish the job, and with a band of picked men, entered her Villa.

This time there were enough men to accomplish the deed. When Agrippina's servants realised what was about to happen they fled.

She recognised Anicetus and with great dignity she said:

"Hast thou come to see me. Then go, tell my son that I am already recovered. Hast thou come to slay me? Then I say it is not my son who commissioned thee."

Instead of answering her, the ship Captain Anicetus struck her on the head with a stick.

"See!" said the Empress, "strike the womb that bore the monster!"

Those were the last words she spoke. The men struck her and struck her until she was dead.

Nero wanted to be sure his mother was dead this time, and had her servants uncover her body, and he stood looking down at it, praising some parts of her body, and decrying other parts, with no feelings at all.

Eventually her servants burnt her corpse in the garden of her Villa, but Nero never had a tomb erected for his mother.

On the morning following Agrippina's death, Nero became very melancholic, and this continued in the form of bad nightmares, and hallucinations.

His behaviour got worse, and his mind became more and more depraved.

He appeared in the company of the greatest debauchees, and he committed sodomy, with many of those who wanted to gain his favour. He especially enjoyed the company of Sporus, who he dressed like a woman.

He would sometimes dress up in skins of wild beasts. He would satisfy his horrendous desires upon men and women alike, who were tied, stark naked, to posts.

Then he would do the same to his slaves.

Nero at this time began to take up singing at all hours of the day and night, and he even announced that he could be hired for performances.

When he was 22 years old his beard was to be shaved off. He made a great fuss of this event, and ordered a Festival to be called Juvenalia.

A great number of invitations were sent out to people to take part in this Festival whatever their age or sex.

Hundreds of people turned up and Nero strutted amongst them. There was pipe playing and dancing and Chariots were raced on the stage.

Nero was excited and screamed and sang.

He moved among the crowd throwing them costly gems, giving those who caught them, horses, chariots and gold and silver cups.

Nero divorced Octavia, although it was some time since the death of Agrippina, who had been so against it.

Twelve days later he married Poppaea.

But Poppaea was evil like Nero. She was insecure whilst Octavia was alive, so she persuaded Nero to have Octavia killed.

She was bound up, and her veins were opened.

She lost a lot of blood and fainted . Then she was put into a vapour bath, where she was stifled. Her head was cut off and then sent to Poppaea.

Within a year of their marriage Nero was presented with a daughter, who he named Augusta. When the child died, he devoted a Temple to her name, a priest and divine honours.

Nero's behaviour became even more strange.

He walked about when he was not singing, with a light scarf round his throat.

He laboured to increase the volume of his voice.

He practised from morning to night, and even lay for hours on his back with a sheet of lead on his chest, to develop his chest muscles.

He consumed vast quantities of leeks and oil on the days before he performed, thinking that they would help him. He never ate anything else on the day.

Nero went to Naples, to sing, as he was prepared to conquer the world with song. He had a most enthusiastic reception and sang for days on end.

He did not even take a bath, and had his meals in the Orchestra, apologising to the crowd for a pause in the proceedings.

Once whilst he was performing there was an earthquake which shook the theatre. Nero just kept on singing through it all, and received tumultuous applause at the end.

But after the theatre was cleared of both performers and spectators, it collapsed having been shaken by the earthquake.

Nero took this as a good sign that the gods were well pleased with him.

He eventually returned to Rome and in the summer night of the 19th July fire broke out in wooden sheds near the Circus Maximus where large stores of spices and oils were kept.

The summer had been hot and dry, and a light breeze carried the flames through the whole area of the sheds.

The fire spread quickly and people were more interested in saving their own possessions than stopping the spread of it.

It is not known whether the fire was spread deliberately on Nero's instructions or because some of the men excited by the events, helped to spread it by setting fire to homes and shops.

The fire lasted for several days and nights, and many homes were lost or plundered.

Nero was at Antium at the time the fire started but on hearing the news he travelled to Rome and went to the highest point of his Palace to view the flames.

He was so thrilled by the fire that he dressed in a fancy costume, picked up his lyre, chanted verses of Homer and sang at the top of his voice.

Only four of the fourteen regions of the City of Rome remained after the fire. It was felt by the people that Nero had ordered the fire, in order to have the chance to rebuild Rome in great splendour.

The Emperor now felt that the people were turning against him.

So he thought that the suspicions of his people should be diverted. He punished with the most terrible tortures the people who professed themselves to be 'Christians'.

These 'Christians' tended to mix only with each other, and to keep secret meetings, and this inflamed the Romans.

On Nero's orders they were treated as sport. They were covered in skins and worried to death by wild dogs, nailed to crosses, or burnt to death.

People rushed to the arenas to see the 'flaming human torches'. These were Christians, their bodies covered in pitch and wax, who were set alight.

Nero enjoyed enormously the outrage, and ran around screaming and singing. He then put on a green costume, got in an ivory Chariot, and rode round and round the arena, with nymphs waving wreaths and scattering incense.

Stakes were driven through men, limbs were broken

73

under chariot wheels, and many other appalling atrocities.

Eventually the people began to feel sorry for the Christians, and realised that their 'evil deeds' were invented by Nero. He panicked and left Rome when he realised that people were blaming him.

He hid himself at Baiae.

Rome was rebuilt and Nero saw to it that he had a magnificent palace of unsurpassed splendour.

About this time a Comet appeared to hang over Rome, which alarmed Nero. He consulted an Astrologer and was told it foretold the death of an eminent person of State.

So Nero slaughtered many noble Romans, to appease the menace of the Star.

Because of his evil deeds, plots to assassinate Nero were becoming more and more common. Many conspirators were found out, and were brought before him.

They then turned on their accusers and denounced them. They too were put to death.

Thousands were butchered on the whim of the Emperor, for any small misdemeanour.

In a fit of rage, Nero kicked his wife Poppaea, whilst she was pregnant. She fell onto the floor, from the wound and died.

Her body was embalmed and buried, which was very unusual as normally Romans were cremated.

Nero became more and more frenzied. Those around him, if they were not murdered, committed suicide, rather than remain with him.

Nero eventually with the help of Epaphroditus, killed himself on the 9th June A.D. 68.

Even in death he was a terrible sight. He had little eyes, a fat throat and chin, a thick neck and great belly, and small thin legs.

His eyes were staring and there was horror and despair on his face, the face of a monster.

He was thirty years of age, and had reigned for fourteen years.

He was the last of the family of Caesars, and the last of the divine Julian Race.

EMPEROR NERO

TZAR ALEXANDER III

Alexander III was a giant. When he was thirty-six years old and came to the throne he was very proud of his physical strength.

He could bend an iron poker over his knees, tear a pack of cards in half and crush a silver rouble with his bare hands.

Everyone who saw him thought his eyes were strange and expressionless and he moved in a particularly ungainly way.

He was German but he had the look of a Russian peasant.

This was how he liked to think of himself, for he grew a beard and wore the check blouses and the baggy trousers of the muzhiks.

The first thing Alexander did on coming to the throne was to tear up the unsigned manifesto lying on his father's desk.

This had made provision for a limited form of Representative Government at a National level.

Alexander's reign began with the persecution of the Jews which was appallingly cruel.

In the reign of Catherine the Great the Jews had been confined to territories on the Western and Southern parts of the Empire.

Under Alexander II however, they had been allowed to expand to all parts of Russia.

Now the new Tzar proclaimed that one third of the Jews in Russia must die, one third emigrate and one third assimilate.

Thousands and thousands of Jews were murdered and their property confiscated.

Alexander really believed that an enormous plot was being organised by international Jewry which intended to end the Monarchy all over the world.

He never spoke of 'Jews' but always said 'Yids'.

His 'May Laws' which were published the following year became famous all over Europe.

A Jew could only leave the place of settlement where they were allowed to live in exceptional circumstances.

No Jew could hold an administrative post, become a Lawyer or own land.

All Jewish schools were to be closed and no Jewish books were to be printed in Hebrew.

A Jew could not marry a Christian unless he gave up his religion, and no Jew could appeal against any sentence of any Court.

In the six months following the publication of these laws it was estimated that 225,000 destitute Jewish families left Russia for Western Europe.

The Emperor was overjoyed.

"Let them carry their poison where they will," he told everyone.

The persecution continued for the next decade.

The Emperor's brother in 1892, the Grand Duke Serge, a sadist and a homosexual, evicted thousands of Jewish artisans and traders from Moscow.

In the middle of the night their quarter was surrounded by mounted Cossacks while policemen ransacked every house.

Someone who was there wrote:

"Of these unhappy people thus driven from their beds and hauled off to prison in the wintry darkness, some were afterwards marched away by *etape,* that is, chained together with criminals and forced along the roads by Cossacks. A few were bribed out of confinement; the rest were summarily shipped away. Today they are scattered— who knows where? over the whole face of the earth . . . There was no charge of criminality or of leading an evil life against any of them."

Alexander's chauvinism did not stop at the Jews.

He took his rustification policy into the Baltic States and Finland, introducing a censorship and making the Russian language compulsory in all the schools.

Even the German families who had settled in Russia since Peter the Great did not escape.

A *ukaz* was issued, aimed at German manufacturers and merchants who built up large businesses.

The Tzar prohibited 'foreigners' from inheriting or acquiring property.

Many were forced to close down their factories and leave.

The German language was forbidden at Court which was something quite new, as all the Tzars had been German.

More important, every man with a German name, who could be replaced by a Russian was thrown out of the Government service.

Tzar Alexander III was frugal to the point of miserliness.

Not only did he cut down on official entertaining, he made economies in food and wine and examined the expenses of his establishments down to the very smallest item.

Soap and candles on his order, must be used up before they were thrown away.

Table linen was not to be changed every day, and lights were not to be left burning in empty rooms.

He decided that twenty people did not require an omelette made with one hundred eggs.

The Tzar's favourite food was cabbage and gruel.

His guests frequently complained that the food in the Palaces was uneatable.

The Emperor's son and heir Nicholas, who was thirteen years old, was so hungry he once opened the gold cross which had been given to him at his baptism and ate the beeswax inside.

TZAR ALEXANDER III

SULTAN MURAD IV AND IBRAHIM I OF
THE OTTOMAN EMPIRE
1640 – 1648

In the Middle Ages, the Turkish Government could always command the services of an Army and Navy of 600,000 men.

But as time passed they could, without the greatest difficulty, raise no more than 300,000.

In 1720 the Janissaries were originally recruited in a very cruel fashion.

Every Christian family in the Provinces which had been conquered by the Ottoman Empire were obliged to give up at least one or two of their male children not over nine years of age to a Commissioner.

He was specially appointed to receive this cruel tribute.

Other children were deliberately kidnapped, while some were saved from those frequently recurring massacres of Christians which became part of Turkish history.

A formidable Army of infant children was annually sent to Constantinople, but a large proportion of them died on the way.

In a great number of cases, parents themselves killed their off-spring rather than let them fall into the hands of the Mohammedans.

When the children eventually arrived, there was an examination to go through.

Those reported to be strong and well-shaped were distributed to certain *Serais* or Barracks.

Those who were weaklings were sold as slaves, or else they were killed.

The more fortunate were educated in the principles of Islam and at the end of five years, drafted into Regiments to commence their Military education.

Every seven years, those who had died were replaced.

The rank and file were, until the reign of Suleyman, never allowed to marry, and each inhabited his own private cell.

They were, however, granted an enormous number of privileges, and early in the history of Turkey they organised themselves into a secret society.

The Officers were allowed to marry on promotion and so exalted was the Agha of the Janissaries that it was possible for him to marry into the Imperial family.

At about the end of the 16th century, the Janissaries began to show signs of insubordination and as the Empire grew more feeble in its administration, the Janissaries became correspondingly more powerful.

They refused to entertain any sort of reform and their lack of discipline made them the scourge of the whole country.

Baron de Tott wrote:

"The mere sight of a Janissary makes the people fly to escape from their insolent brutality."

However, every European merchant was obliged by law to keep a Janissary attached to his service.

In the Seraglio there was an ill-omened courtyard, known as the Court of the Janissaries, where they had their merry-makings in times of peace and victory.

They behaved like a horde of terrible savages, beating their drums and kettles.

Their wild cries would rend the air as they clamoured for the disposition of the Sultan or demanded largesse.

In 1623, Sultan Murad IV (Ghazi the Victorious) put to death tens of thousands of bandits during the first five months of his reign.

In Constantinople, those who were not careful to move in 'the path of righteousness and orthodoxy' were in imminent danger of falling into the hands of this Ottoman 'Pedro the Cruel.'

A picture of what occurred of the tricks and manner of the Sultan is that when he was 'in his cups' he was insupportable.

He put to death the Pashas of greatest note and confiscated their estates to his Exchequer.

Whereas avarice and cruelty were equally predominant in his nature, there was scarcely a day when he did not make some demonstration of these dispositions.

He took singular delight to sit in a kiosk by the seaside and shoot at people with his bow and arrows as they rowed near the banks of the Seraglio.

This caused the boatmen ever afterwards to keep themselves at a safe distance from the walls.

It was also his custom to go from one garden to another along the Bosphoros to see if there was anybody bold enough to look out and see him pass.

If discovered, his curiosity was repaid when the Sultan shot him with his carbine.

"It cannot be expressed," someone wrote, "the dread and fear in which the people stood of him."

This agreeable Sultan, like his hated successor, lived in terror of assassination and conspiracy.

He would go out at night with his boon companion, a renegade Italian, and, incognito, visit the lowest taverns.

If he caught a man smoking, he once revealed himself by cutting off the man's head.

On one occasion he caught one of his gardeners and his wife smoking.

He ordered them to be seized, had their legs cut off and exhibited their bodies in a public place until they died.

In the last year of his reign, all lights had, on the point of death, to be extinguished an hour after sunset.

In 1635 he had 75,000 of his subjects executed.

In 1640, after a long drinking bout, Murad died aged only twenty-eight.

Even as he realised he could no longer live, he ordered his brother Ibrahim, who was his successor to be murdered.

When his mother told him the order had been carried out, Murad, smiling, sank back on his cushions and died.

But his mother had been lying and Ibrahim became the next Sultan.

Ibrahim I was one of the most detestable of all the

Turkish Sovereigns.

In the midst of one of his debaucheries, he had the idea of tying *all* the women of his Seraglio up in sacks.

They were seized, in the dead of night, thrust into bags that were weighted down by stones and thrown into the Bosphoros.

It was something that had happened before in Turkey, but never so many woman all at one time.

However, by a miracle, one of them escaped, floated and was picked up at sea by a European vessel, and finally brought to Paris.

When she told the tale of her terrible experience it was finally calculated that between two-hundred and three-hundred women had been sent to the bottom of the sea in the traditional sack.

It was an easy way in Turkey to get rid of troublesome wives and slaves without fear of detection.

Not even an Inspector of Police might enter a Harem under any pretext, nor enquire as to what took place within it.

The Sultans had a completely free hand to do as they wished, however cruel, however terrifying.

Ibrahim I has gone down in history as being the only Sultan to dispose of his entire Harem in one night.

SULTAN MURAD IV

KING ALFONSO XIII OF SPAIN

H.M. KING ALFONSO XIII OF SPAIN
1886 – 1941

King Alfonso of Spain was not only unlucky in his number but he was also reputed and believed by his subjects to have "The Evil Eye".

They had some reason for this idea because both his sons died in car crashes and following that the most appalling things happened when King Alfonso paid an official visit to Italy in 1932.

The misfortunes which were connected with him spiritually began even before the Monarch ever stepped ashore.

Several sailors in the flotilla sent to greet him were washed over-board and drowned.

This was followed by an explosion in one of the submarines accompanying the ship.

The very moment that King Alfonso set foot on Italian soil an ancient cannon which was fired in his honour, blew up killing as it did so, the entire crew.

To make matters worse and to emphasise to the public the danger of even the slightest contact with the King of Spain, a Naval Officer with whom he had shaken hands, collapsed and died very shortly afterwards.

Now of course, the whole of Italy was talking, speculating and waiting with a feeling of horror, for the next disaster.

In fact no one was surprised, when on the King's tour of Lake Gleno, the dam burst, killing fifty people and making five hundred homeless.

Mussolini was so overcome by King Alfonso's reputation, that he refused to meet him. He conducted all negotiations through an intermediary regardless of how insulting it must have seemed to his guest.

FREDERICK WILLIAM I OF PRUSSIA

FREDERICK WILLIAM I OF PRUSSIA

Frederick William I had two crazes — one of these was avarice, the other the formation of a corps of giant soldiers.

Every year of his reign he put away a large sum of money and at the same time ransacked the world for giants for his Army.

He paid £1,300 to induce an Irish giant of seven feet high to enlist.

Not content with the giants he had under him he started to breed them like horses or cattle.

Whenever he saw a tall young woman he had her married forcibly to one of his tallest soldiers.

King William riding one day in the forests came upon a beautiful girl of about six feet in height.

She did not know the King by sight, but he got into conversation with her and offered her a thaler or two to carry a note for him.

She agreed good-humouredly to his request.

The note was to the Officer commanding the guard at a fortress not far distant, and ran as follows:

"Instantly have the bearer of this letter married to Corporal Fritz of the Grenadiers."

The King rode away in one direction while the girl went off in the other.

As she walked on she realised that if she was to accomplish her mission she would be compelled to miss an appointment that afternoon with her lover.

She suddenly remembered an old crone who lived alone in a hut on the borders of the forest.

She gave the old woman half of the King's bounty and begged her to take the note to the Officer at the fortress.

The old crone agreed and the girl hurried away eagerly in search of her lover.

When King William rode into the fortress in the evening it was to find the Corporal married, but to an old hag.

The Kingdom of Prussia merely dated from the year 1701

and during his reign of twenty-seven years from 1713, the King increased his dominions of what had been the Electorate of Brandenburg by the conquest from Charles XII of Pomerania, with Stettin and the islands at the mouth of the Oder.

He was married to Sophia Dorothea of Hanover, daughter of George I of England, and among her ten children the eldest son, Prince Frederick, and a daughter, Wilhelmina, incurred the ferocious hatred of their father.

The King tried to make the Prince renounce the succession, which young Frederick agreed to do — provided the King would declare that he was not his father.

From childhood to the age of twenty, King Frederick William vented his rage upon the youth in the most savage manner.

But the Prince who had been brought up by French refugees had a strong passion for French literature.

He was not, however, allowed to learn Latin, Greek, English or any other language.

After narrowly escaping death at his father's hands, Frederick attempted to escape to his Uncle George II in England.

He was captured and sentenced to death as a deserter.

The King, having executed before his son's eyes a young officer who has assisted in his flight, kept the Prince a prisoner at Cästrin before carrying out upon him the sentence of death also.

In the meantime, however, the Emperor, the Kings of Sweden and Poland, and the rulers of the United States of Holland, contrived by their interposition to save the Prince.

After a long imprisonment he was banished from the Court to Rheinsberg, when his father forced him to marry Elizabeth Christina, daughter of the Duke of Brunswick Bevern, in 1733.

Various stories are told of his youthful excesses, but he could never have been, as they pretended, a monster of vice.

At Rheinberg Frederick followed his literary tastes and collected around him French and German savants.

Now left in peace he played the flute without fear of the instrument being broken over his head.

He dined without danger of having dishes flung at him, and was able to sit undisturbed to write verses and prose without expecting the apparition of a furious father, to drag him round by the hair of his head while kicking him with heavy riding-boots.

While Frederick was writing the *Anti-Macchiavelli* and many other of his celebrated works, his crazy old father's heart was becoming softened towards him.

He died after sobbing out upon his son's breast the words, "My God, my God, I die content with such a noble son to succeed me."

KING HENRY III OF FRANCE

KING HENRY III OF FRANCE
1551 – 1589

King Henry, King of France had originally been King of Poland.

However in 1574 his brother Charles IX died, and Henry succeeded to the French throne.

He arrived in Paris but the French stared at him in amazement.

It was not just that his cheeks were rouged nor was it that his hair and beard were dyed and scented with violet powder.

Nor were they particularly overwhelmed by the emerald and pearl pendant earrings that he wore.

What was so astonishing was that he dressed in a gown of pink damask with billowing sleeves tied with gold thread.

The Courtiers tied to reassure each other that the new King's costume was a fancy dress specially designed for the occasion.

It was impossible however, to disguise the truth.

King Henry's costume was only an exaggerated form of his every day dress.

He did not put on a skirt but he usually wore feminine clothes, powdered and painted his face, carried a fan and was festooned in jewellery.

He curled his hair every day and exchanged beauty tips with his wife Louise.

Every night he slept in a cosmetic face mask.

Just occasionally he felt remorse for his vanity and as a penance he would go bare-footed to Church whipping himself as he walked there and wearing only sack-cloth to cover his sensitive skin.

However remorsed he might feel, within two or three days he was dressed up once again in his glamorous garments preening himself in front of his boyfriends.

Apart from his appearance which occupied a great deal of his time, he fussed over his lap-dogs which numbered two thousand.

They too lived a life of splendour and his favourites among them were especially pampered and slept each night in a velvet cushioned apartment next to the Royal bed-chamber.

King Henry was so obsessed by his animals that when he went for a walk he could not bear to leave any behind.

It was his idea to build a large light basket, richly lined with crimson silk which would accommodate thirty dogs who were then carried behind their Master whenever he went for a walk.

What he loathed were cats.

In fact, he developed such a fear of them that he fainted if one came near him.

With so much to occupy his mind, he attended only occasionally to affairs of State.

It was a blessing that in 1589 a patriot assassinated him.

CAIUS CAESAR "CALIGULA"
12 – 41 A.D.

Caius Caesar, the son of Germanicus and Agrippina was born on the 31st August in the year A.D. 12, at a place called Antium.

He spent his childhood in the camp on the Moselle and the Rhine. He was given the name 'Caligula' or 'Little Boots' by the soldiers who saw him strut about in stout military sandals, laced to above the ankles.

He was seven years old when his father died, so he went to live with his mother until her arrest, eventually finishing up at the home of his grandmother, Antonia.

Because neither his mother nor his grandmother knew how to handle the strong-willed child, he was allowed to run riot.

Eventually due to his misbehaviour, he was taken to Capri where he remained until he ascended to the throne in A.D. 37.

Throughout his childhood Caligula had epileptic fits. Although he outgrew them, he still had sudden fainting spells and extreme fluctuations of temper from depression to sheer rage, the rest of his life.

Whilst on Capri he was befriended by a Jew named Herod Agrippa who was twice his age. He taught him about the customs of the East.

But Caligula was not prepared for the throne as his father had been. Germanicus had been taught self-discipline, the way to command others, and he had attended the Senate.

However Caligula had none of this training, much preferring to go his own way.

One day Herod and Caligula were out driving together when Herod remarked that he hoped it would not be long before the Emperor died.

The remark was overheard by the Charioteer, and, when arrested for theft, begged to be brought before the Emperor Tiberius.

The Emperor realised that the servant spoke the truth, and he arrested Herod, who was kept in prison until old Tiberius died.

To make amends to his friend, Caligula made Herod King of a portion of Judaea.

In the first year of his reign Caligula fell dangerously ill, and the crowds waited outside his Palace, expecting news of his death.

But Caligula recovered, although he was never the same, and his mind seemed to have undergone a dramatic change.

He began to suffer from want of sleep. He seldom had more than three or four hours a night, and when he did he had very frightening dreams.

He was so terrified by them that he would sit up in bed experiencing wild fantasies or else wander about his Palace.

At the time of his sickness he had drawn up his Will, in favour of his second sister Drusilla, and made her the heiress of his property and of the Empire.

Although Drusilla had been married to Longinus by Tiberius, Caligula divorced them, and married her to one of his own friends Lepidus.

He then took her from Lepidus, and declared that he loved her so much, he would marry her himself.

This scandalised Rome.

His grandmother Antonia remonstrated with him, but he told her:

"Everything is lawful to me, and I may do as I will to anyone."

He was eventually dissuaded but he then refused to speak to his grandmother and threw her servants into prison.

Antonia died, and whether it was by poison or by suicide is not known, but certainly Caligula was instrumental in her death. He watched disinterestedly as her body was burned on a funeral pyre, laughing and drinking with his friends.

Caligula considered himself divine, and if the Pharaohs of Egypt could marry their sisters, he could do the same.

Medals and cameos were made with the heads of both Caligula and Drusilla together.

But Drusilla became ill and died.

Caligula was frenzied with grief, gave orders for an extravagant funeral and decreed that thereafter she would be called Panthea (the All-Goddess) and worshipped like Venus.

Unable to rest in his Villa, the mad Emperor roamed through the cities of Italy and Sicily. He let his hair and beard grow in a token of sorrow.

On the day on which young Tiberius, Caligula's cousin, entered his nineteenth year, Caligula adopted him, believing by doing so he had the right of a father over a son, and could control the boy.

But Tiberius was delicate with a bad cough.

Because Caligula could smell cough mixture on his breath, he tormented him by saying he had taken an antidote to poison.

He made his life such an unspeakable misery that young Tiberius took a sword, and asking a Tribune how to do it, he threw himself on it.

Macro who had been a great friend of his grandfather, also tutored Caligula. But Caligula got tired of the old man's wise counsel.

"I am a boy no more," Caligula said to his courtiers. "Look at the man, he conducts himself as though still my tutor."

Macro's fate was sealed. He killed his wife and then committed suicide.

Caligula made sure that his children were also killed.

The next person who was threatening to the Emperor, was his father-in-law Junius Silanus.

Caligula resented the advice he gave him and to save the confiscation of all his goods by the Emperor, Silanus cut his own throat with a razor.

Caligula had been married to Junia Claudilla in Capri, but she died, and in the first year of his reign he was invited to the wedding of Caius Piso with Livia Orestilla.

He took a fancy to the bride himself and ran off with her, but divorced her after only a few days, then banished her from his kingdom.

Someone told him that the famous beauty Lollia was like her Grandmother, and that she possessed the most magnificent set of jewels of any Roman lady.

However, after marrying her, he rapidly tired of her and also divorced her.

He was then attracted to Caesonia, the mother of three daughters, and married her. He was surprised by the strength of his attachment for her. Yet sometimes he would touch her neck and say:

"When I give the word, this beautiful throat will be hacked through."

Then he would laugh hysterically.

Shortly after their marriage Caesonia gave birth to a daughter whom Caligula called Julia Drusilla.

When he saw her biting her nurse, or flying at another child, trying to scratch its eyes out, he would applaud her, saying there was little doubt she was his daughter.

Caligula was becoming very irrational, and every tenth day a list of prisoners was brought to him, so he could condemn them to death, — "to clear the account."

Sometimes he would not even look at the list, but just raise his hand, signifying the death of them all.

The money left by his grandfather Emperor Tiberius when he died, was soon squandered by Caligula, who then set about plundering the rich by confiscating their goods and taxing them heavily. If they protested they were put to death.

He told everyone he was in touch with the gods, and each day he would pretend to be a different god.

One day he would appear with wings and say he was Mercury, on another day he would carry a bow and quiver and be Apollo.

He would be surrounded by attendants, all dressed as

the ministers of the deity he was impersonating that particular day.

There was only one thing Caligula loved more than himself and that was his horse *Incitatus*.

He would visit the horse each morning, talk to him in a sickly voice, and place garlands of flowers round his neck.

Incitatus had a marble stall built especially for him, containing a beautiful ivory manger with purple housings, and a jewelled front.

Caligula took his horse with him everywhere, kissing and cuddling him. He insisted that his friends treated the horse with more respect than was received by any of his wives.

Incitatus had his own servants, and was fed with the best and finest food.

Caligula even wanted the horse to be made a member of the Senate, but eventually he was persuaded that this was not possible.

He was furious and threw himself into a raging fury, which lasted for weeks.

For four years Rome was ruled by Caligula during which time they were shocked by his association with his sister, his pretence at being a god, his execution of a great number of Senators and Knights, the way he plundered property to meet his own extravagances and how he adored and almost worshipped his horse.

The final straw was the way he antagonised his Armies, more especially his own body-guards.

Eventually a plot was hatched to assassinate the Tyrant.

In A.D. 41 the Palatine Games were to take place in January, and to last for eight days. The Games culminated on the last day with a play.

Caligula sat in a box on the stage to watch the proceedings.

At luncheon time it was suggested to him that as the rest of the performance could not continue until dark, he might like a bath.

A procession started and Caligula entered a passage near

the bath house. He talked to some youths from Greece and Asia Minor, who were performing in the play.

As he went nearer the bath-house a Tribune struck him with a sword, between the neck and shoulder, a second blow struck his jaw. Joined by further conspirators, he received more than thirty wounds.

Reports varied as to whether he was dead or injured and as people returned to their seats, rumours went round the theatre.

Then the public Orator took black clothes from the theatrical wardrobe and announced that Caius Caesar was dead.

The conspirators then worried about the influence of Caligula's wife Caesonia and his daughter Julia. So that they could not cause any trouble, they killed them both.

"Little Boots" died on January 24th at the age of twenty-eight, having reigned tyranically for only three years, ten months and eight days.

CALIGULA

H.M. KING FERDINAND IV

H.M. KING FERDINAND IV
1751 – 1825

King Ferdinand IV King of the two Sicilies ruled over Naples.

Before the King was eighteen Marquis Tanucci, then Prime Minister, was sent from the Court at Madrid to find a wife for the King.

The young lady chosen was the Archduchess Josepha, one of the daughters of the Empress Maria Theresa.

Word was sent to Ferdinand that she was bright, intelligent and attractive and she would make him an excellent Queen.

The King waited for her with eager anticipation and even impatience.

He was therefore upset when he received news that she had died in Vienna from smallpox.

At least, that is to say that he showed as much concern as could be expected from a King, when he had not even met the young lady.

But he felt even more upset when it was suggested to him that he ought not go out hunting and fishing on the day he had heard such sad news.

The King, after some argument, reluctantly agreed that it would not be prudent to seem so heartless and decided to find other pleasures in the Palace instead.

He gathered his Courtiers round about him and they started by playing billiards, a game the King enjoyed very much, and at which he was extremely skilled.

After he had played it for some time, he ordered that it should be followed by a game of leap-frog, and then with various other indoor games.

Later on when he was bored, he suggested that he and his friends ought to pay their respects to the dead Archduchess, by having a funeral for her.

After much discussion the King chose one of the Chamberlains who was young and rather feminine in appearance.

They dressed him in mournful feminine clothes, laid him out on an open bier as was the custom in Naples at the time, so that the ceremony was correct in every detail. The King then marked his hands and face with chocolate drops to imitate the smallpox marks.

When the King had made sure he was satisfied with everything, the Procession started and proceeded through the principal apartments of the Palace and out into the grounds, with King Ferdinand as Chief Mourner.

QUEEN JUANA OF CASTILLE

Queen Juana was married to Philip I and despite the fact that he did not treat her well, first of all by his infidelities and then by imprisoning her, Juana was deeply in love with her husband.

Philip was very handsome and the Queen was extremely jealous of him.

When he was taken ill Juana kept vigil by his bed by day and by night, and personally took charge of nursing him.

No matter what she did she could not save him and she was overcome with grief when he finally died.

She did not cry at all, but just sat in a darkened room without moving, with her head in her hands.

The Queen decided she could not be parted from her husband so she had his body embalmed and placed in a coffin which she took everywhere with her.

Each night as it grew dark the coffin was always placed where she could see it from her window, and she would sit and stare at it.

At the end of a year she came to the decision that she must have her husband buried and ordered it to be carried out in Granada.

The coffin was put on a most magnificent carriage to be drawn by four horses and a great procession of Churchmen and Nobles left Burgos.

They were only allowed to journey by night because Queen Juana said:

"As a widow my soul has been extinguished. I must remain in the dark!"

At every stopping place the coffin was taken to either a Church or a Monastery where it remained all day, and where a Funeral Service was held, as if the King had just died.

The Queen had ordered a large bodyguard for the coffin in order to protect it from women, because although Philip had been dead for a year, she was still jealous, and would not let women near his coffin.

In fact on one occasion when they stopped the coffin was placed in a Nunnery, in mistake for a Monastery.

When she realised what had happened Queen Juana was furious and she ordered that the coffin be removed immediately to a field some distance away.

She was so passionately jealous of her handsome husband that she then insisted that the coffin was unsealed so that she could make sure the Nuns had not robbed her of any single part of her husband.

When she was satisfied she camped beside the coffin in the field.

The journey continued with the Queen in her dark, dirty clothes, and her father Ferdinand was horrified when he saw her appearance and persuaded her to go to the Castle of Tordesillas.

King Philip was finally buried in the Monastery and so Queen Juana could look out of her window at the tomb of her husband.

The remains of Philip were eventually taken to Granada and placed in the Cathedral Church and Queen Juana, when she died was placed beside her husband and a sepulchre was built by their son Charles V for them to rest in peace.

QUEEN JUANA OF CASTILLE

KUBLAI KHAN

KUBLAI KHAN
1215 – 1294

Kublai Khan, Emperor of China, went to extraordinary lengths to ensure that each of his concubines were fit to share his bed.

He devised an almost unbelievably complicated method of ensuring that the girls were unspoilt before they came to him.

The selection began two years before the girl was actually required by the Emperor.

Agents were sent out with detailed specifications to scour the Tartar province of Ungut, where the women were reputed to be the most beautiful in all China.

They would collect several hundred girls who were then taken to a certain place to be examined.

There, the weeding out ceremony began, and of the hundreds originally picked, only a mere dozen or so would be accepted.

Those who did the judging were all men who had made a close study of the female form.

It had now become a serious academic procedure where the girls were evaluated in carats, just like precious stones.

Each feature, hair, mouth, face, teeth, legs and no doubt other parts of their bodies were appraised separately and given a certain number of carats.

When these were totalled up the girls who were awarded twenty to twenty-four carats were carried off to the Court for the next stage.

It was then that Kublai Khan came to see them for himself.

He would look the girls over and more would be eliminated, leaving only about thirty or forty to take the final test.

This was most vigorous and searching.

First they were subjected to a physical inspection to ensure that no man had touched them.

They were then placed in the care of a Noble's wife whose task it was to see that they had no irritating habits or so far undiscovered imperfections.

It was a full time operation, for the wives had to sleep with the girls to make sure they did not snore, or suffer from unpleasant bodily odours.

The girls who survived all this scrutiny were then chosen as part of the new intake of the Khan's Harem.

They then shared the Emperor's bed, and he always had them in it in bunches of five.

They would cater to his every whim for three days and nights after which the next five came on duty.

In this way he managed to father forty-seven sons and innumerable daughters.

His way of living did not shorten his life.

Waited on by servants who stuffed silken napkins into their mouths so as not to contaminate his food with their low-born breath he lived to the age of seventy-nine. This was an incredible age to reach in the 17th century.

WILLIAM II THE KAISER, KING OF PRUSSIA AND THE GERMAN EMPEROR
1859 – 1941

William II, who was always known as The Kaiser was extremely niggardly, in fact it became an obsession with him.

He was very generous to himself and expected the best of everything and his egotism grew and grew as he became older.

Those who waited on him personally, like his Valets, received fifty *marks* from their Imperial Master as a Christmas gratuity.

All his other servants, men and women, had to be content with ten *marks* 'for gingerbread,' as the *pourboire* was styled in Court.

"And that is the only '*Trinkgeld*' the Kaiser dispenses all the year round," the wife of one of the wardrobemen complained. "Outside Christmas His Majesty never seemed to have a *pfennig* for his body-servants."

Although the Kaiser was in constant need of stimulants several times a day, it never occurred to him while he was tucking into four or five cognacs in the course of the day that his overworked attendants might feel like stepping across the way to the Canteen to 'crook an arm.'

Beggars who accosted him on his rides through Potsdam or Berlin received three *marks* from the Emperor.

A like sum was appropriated every Sunday for the benefit of the contribution-plate.

His Adjutant handed him a coin before he stepped into his carriage going to Church.

The treatment of his servants appalled a beholder who was brave enough to write *"The Secret History of the Court of Berlin."*

She found forty hungry women and girls, some old, many young and pretty hanging about the back stairs of what is intended for the most magnificent Royal Court of the day.

Some of them munched black bread, scantily spread with lard, while they drank from tin bottles draughts of cold chicory masquerading under the name of coffee.

One or two clasped a hunk of salt pork, but many of them depended upon the charity of their colleagues, or the good nature of the liveried servants for a meal.

They wore washed-out calico dresses all the year round and a twenty-four by forty-inch shawl barely covering their heads and breasts in Winter.

Yet they were Imperial and Royal employees, the same title as those of Her Majesty's smart maids, in gold and silver dresses.

The only difference was that the smart maids were employed by the year, while the other women were employed by the month during Their Majesty's stay at the Court of Potsdam.

The allowances for the Royal board were cut so fine that it only just sufficed for their Majesties, the *entourage,* and the guests.

When the Kaiser invited company at the last moment the courses had to be hastened to cover up the shortage of food.

Often the Royal guests left the flower-strewn table almost as hungry as the scrub-girls did.

The women who lived in or near Potsdam worked in the Castle from six in the morning until six, and sometimes eight at night, many walking an hour or more to and from their destination.

They were employed in the apartments of the Adjutants, of the Ladies and Gentlemen of the Court in the servants' quarters, and in the kitchens, cleaning, scrubbing, wood and water-carrying.

Even so, the two-hundred room Palace had no kitchen where they could cook a scanty meal or a room in which they could eat and rest.

"They get their wages — what more do they want?" the

House-marshals replied when asked about this.

Their wages were in fact two *marks* per day for twelve or fourteen hours' work, and even in the coldest Winter could not get a cup of coffee or a plate of soup, although it is obvious they could not go home for dinner recess.

The brave Author who wrote of what she found in the Kaiser's Palace said that it gave her a shock every time she saw 'these pariahs of our splendid Court fighting hunger and cold with food devoid of warmth, behind doors and staircases where the wind whistles the international anthem of poverty.'

Bearing in mind the Kaiser and Kaiserin's predilection of cleanliness, the difficulties of the exchequer occasionally interfered with this.

Their Majesties were therefore sometimes unable to obtain clean sheets for their bed and the servants were kept very short of towels and bed-clothes.

In fact, the bed-linen was changed only once a month, while the liveried retainers were supposed to be paragons of cleanliness.

One evening the Author of *'The Secret History of the Court of Berlin'* was talking to Her Majesty and one of the Ladies made the remark that Prince Frederick Leopold compelled his Valets to bathe two or three times a day, morning, noon and night, and always before they came into personal contact with him.

"That is extravagant," said Her Majesty, "but persons of our rank cannot insist too strongly upon the daily bath for their attendants."

"If there are enough bath-rooms!" the Author could not resist saying.

"I suppose there is a sufficient number in *our* Palaces," the Kaiserin remarked, "especially here in the Schloss."

"I beg Your Majesty's pardon," the Author said in reply, "here, as well as in Berlin, you have but two bath-rooms for servants — one for the men, one for the women."

The Empress gave her a startled look.

"Two bath-rooms?"

"Two," the Author repeated, "and not only the people of the body-service, but all the liveried and uniformed men and women in the Palace-coachmen, *fourriers,* chauffeurs, and heads of the household departments are expected to use them."

"*Meine Liebe,*" the Empress replied, "you are evidently misinformed."

The Author wondered afterwards what Her Majesty would have thought if she had continued with her revelations.

She had discovered that the servants' wash-bowls were little tin affairs, holding less than three pints.

The toilets for the servants were located on the back-stair landings, which were lighted by kerosene lamps day and night, and one closet had to do for every twenty-six people.

She was aware that a command from the Emperor or the Empress could have changed this disgraceful state of affairs.

Since William II had come to the throne the German people had paid 160-million *marks* into the Civil List.

Of this, 100-millions were expected to keep up the pageant of superficial splendour that goes to make a Court.

When the Housekeeper was asked to increase the small allowance of linen given to the servants, she answered:

"I would like to, but I cannot, as funds for labour and material in the wash-kitchen just cover the stipulated amount of laundry. Half-a-dozen extra towels per week would upset calculations. When the household linen is given out on Saturdays, the presses are as empty as the proverbial nutshell."

When the Prince of Wales visited Berlin in March, 1889 his employees, from valet down to groom, were constantly brawling with those in charge of the Kitchens because they were given what they called a 'starvation diet.'

When the typical German breakfast consisting of coffee, milk, two rolls, a tiny pat of butter, and two pieces of sugar, was sent in to the Valet, he demanded steak and eggs in addition, and so did the footmen and grooms.

These protests were received with silent contempt but when the noon meal called for similar criticisms, it was threatened that His Royal Highness would be informed of the men's 'unruly behaviour.'

"By all means do so," the Englishmen replied, "that is what we want. Our master will then engage board for us at an Hotel. That is the kind of Gentleman he is."

And so the battle waged merrily on.

Only one bottle of beer was allowed to the foreigners, and they asked permission to provide their own drinks.

They refused to eat cold pork and potato-salad for supper and when told it was Her Majesty's favourite dish, their remarks approached dangerously near *lèse-majesté*.

The Prince of Wales's men had a very hard time of it at the Schloss and they were cursed by the servants, in the presence of Her Majesty, as 'the hungriest and most impudent sort of menials' they had ever encountered.

The Emperor was proud of his personal strength and was delighted when a foreign correspondent likened his fist to the 'terrible right' of John L. Sullivan.

His sister remarked:

"I hope Sullivan has not the bad taste to wear as many rings as my brother."

The Kaiser was trying to hide some disfiguring moles on his hands, but the rings only succeeded in emphasising the blemishes.

Few people had a correct idea of the Emperor's height, as he is seldom seen without a helmet culminating in a point.

However, Prince Eitel Fritz once said that his father measured five feet, six inches, although the Kaiserine always said he was five feet, eight.

The Kaiser said he owed his clear complexion and the

possession of a remarkably white and smooth skin to the fact that he used soap of a particular brand since earliest childhood.

In his dressing-room, while there is one photograph of little merit of the Kaiserine, on every table, console and chest-of-drawers there is evidence of the Kaiser's vain passion for seeing himself in pictures.

They portray His Majesty in every variety of costume, on manoeuvres, on the parade-field, hunting, sailing, or making his entry into some town or village amid the loyal shouts of the populace.

WILLIAM II (KAISER)

LE DUC D'ORLEAN

LE DUC D'ORLEAN
BROTHER OF KING LOUIS XIV
d. 1701

The Duke d'Orleans, known as *Monsieur,* had temporary rooms in the Château of 1674 and a much grander Suite when Versailles became even bigger.

His brother King Louis XIV was devoted to him, and until the Dauphin grew up *Monsieur* was the most important person at the Court.

Physically he was a caricature of his brother, three-quarters of his height and more oriental-looking, swarthy with eyes like black olives.

Monsieur, despite being a famous sodomite, had two wives, a mistress and eleven illegitimate children, seven of whom died in infancy, or were born dead.

He is called the 'grandfather of Europe' because every Roman Catholic family has him amongst their ancestors.

All the Kings of France after Louis XIV, as well as Marie-Antoinette and the son of Napoleon descend from him.

He modelled himself on Henri III, even to the point of being devout, although this came from his love of ceremony.

He had been carefully brought up by the Mazarin and Anne of Austria in ignorance of public affairs so that he should not embarrass his brother with political ambitions.

This meant that *Monsieur's* interests in life were clothes, jewels, parties, etiquette, objects of art, and boys.

Monsieur loved his Château at Saint-Cloud, which was perhaps the most attractive of all the Royal country residences.

In his youth *Monsieur* had enjoyed battles.

He always arrived late on the field, having painted and powdered, with all his eyelashes stuck together, his clothes covered with ribbons and diamonds.

He never wore a hat for fear of flattening his wig.

Once in battle he was as brave as a lion, only worried about what the sun and the dust was doing to his complexion.

He however proved an excellent strategist, but he found warfare too exhausting.

He was the only member of his family not to enjoy violent exercise which was why he never went out hunting and in fact never went outdoors if he could help it.

Monsieur could be amusing and he was a chatterbox at family gatherings where his voice could be heard above everybody else's.

The King, who had no small talk, was glad of it and listened with an amused smile on his lips to the nonsense his brother talked.

Monsieur treated the King with respectful familiarity.

He knew his place and he stayed in it.

The King responded affectionately to him, but with, undoubtedly, a hint of condescension.

H.M. QUEEN CHRISTINA OF SWEDEN
1626-1689

The child was ushered from the blazing sunlit passages, to a darkened room where the only light came from two small candles.

As her eyes became accustomed to the gloom she saw that the whole room, walls, ceiling and windows, had been draped in black cloth.

The bed itself was black and her mother lay in it wearing a long black veil. Only her fluttering hands showed white against the prevailing darkness.

The widowed Queen did nothing but groan while Princess Christina timorously advanced towards her.

"Look," the Queen said, "there is the heart that used to beat so powerfully."

Despite the protests of the Lutheran Clergy, Maria Eleanora had insisted on having the body of her husband embalmed and the heart removed.

It was only when Christina began to scream aloud that she desisted from opening the casket and actually putting the heart in the child's hands.

Christina began to cry almost as loudly as her mother, that it was from fear and not from grief did not matter to the woman whose mind had almost given way.

Christina turned from the bed and began to run towards the door.

She started back because of a movement from the shadows.

She thought for a moment she was seeing something supernatural.

In actual fact, it was one of her mother's dwarfs who had been lying asleep.

In the days and weeks that followed, while Christina was forced to obey her mother's commands and enter into the terrible room for a session of perverted sentimental mourning and praying, there was always a dwarf, or some crippled travesty of a human being for her to meet there.

Suddenly in the midst of a moaning dirge for the dead King, the woman in bed would screech:

"Now come and play with the dwarf. He is very strong and very entertaining. He will show you many tricks and unusual games. He is the only friend I have in the world."

The Palace was, of course, aware of what was going on, and eventually they considered the mourning period must be terminated.

There were many hysterical outbursts from that funeral room, but at last the authorities got their way.

The body of King Gustavus Adolphus, still awaiting burial was taken to the great Church in Stockholm and interred with the heart from the golden casket.

That was the last occasion that Queen Maria Eleanora was able to indulge in her delight for parading her grief.

It was also the last time she was able to damage her daughter's mind by that travesty of amusement with her dwarfs.

As soon as the funeral was over the State Council went in formal procession to her room and informed her that on the late King's orders she was no longer to see her child.

"I do not believe it," she stormed. "I have lost my husband to this accursed country, am I now to lose my only child?"

Count Magnus de Gardie had special privileges in the Palaces of Stockholm and Upsala.

He was a cold and calculating man, not particularly enamoured of the inexperienced girl, especially because she had an ugly face and an awkward body.

He regarded himself as a connoisseur of women, as well as everything else.

At the same time, because of what she could give him, as much as he dared, he made his relationship with Christina one of theoretical love-making.

He talked to her of his own exotic adventures and he coloured their discussions on art and literature with a sexual flavour which aroused Christina's desires and accentuated her hunger for love in whatever form it was presented to her.

Before her eyes were opened to his real attitude towards her, she had presented him with estates producing a revenue of the incredible sum of 80,000 rix dollars a year.

Those who understood the real character of the young Count suspected that he was a sadist.

Even those who did not know the word, they knew of his cruel perversions.

If the truth could be revealed, it would probably show that Magnus was as bored with sex as Christina was bewitched by it.

He had the intelligence to realise that fundamentally the young Queen Christina dreaded the day when her heart should rule her brain.

He pandered to this by forming her worst suspicions that sexual love lowered human beings to a bestial level rather than raised them to Divine heights.

If Christina inwardly recoiled in horror from the entertainments the Count arranged for her in the La Gardie Palace, lonely and discreetly distanced from the Capital, she managed to hide it.

She was acutely envious of his worldly knowledge and laughed uproariously to disguise her innocence and trembling revulsion.

Because she thought it would amuse the Count she obtained a collection of improper songs and taught a bevy of girls to sing them parrot-fashion.

The unfortunate songsters, little more than children, had no idea whatever of the obscenities they were mouthing.

Count Magnus's corruption of Christina was extended to the Ambassador of Spain, Con Antonio Pimentelli, a 'Don Juan' who thought the Queen might be interesting.

But the Queen, he found, was no different from other women.

She was the typical willing and, therefore, uninteresting

victim of his charm.

He disguised the truth of his contempt for her because his diplomatic duties demanded it.

Even when the Queen insisted that he move into a suite at the Palace so that they could meet in intimacy whenever she wished, he kept the comedy going.

Pimentelli soon discovered the Queen's liking for bawdy stories and he arranged for his staff to tell him a few jokes before he left every evening for a tête-à-tête in her Palace appartments.

Christina delighted in his poker face as he recited the obscenities of the Stockholm quayside and drinking dens.

She did not realise that to him the stories were insupportably pointless and crude.

Pimentelli made the best of the circumstances.

He was able to increase his own wealth and influence as the doyen of the diplomats in Stockholm.

To other Statesmen he would damn the Queen's womanly attractions by stressing her intellectual abilities.

"She is of an admirable spirit and courage beyond her sex," he once told the English Ambassador. "She is well skilled in Military affairs, and as fit as a woman possibly could be to lead an Army."

Christina later began to have times when she longed to be alone.

She would shut herself in a room walking round and round, soaking herself in its luxury and beauty.

Temporarily at least, her desire for the tantalising attraction of Pimentelli and her hunger for heavy dalliance with undoubtedly low-born hangers on in her retinue had vanished.

She remembered the fleeting happiness that had almost been within her grasp time after time in her adolescence.

Queen Christina began to be tired of Count Magnus just at a time when he found himself falling in love with her.

He was not the only man in her world and she took lovers, several of whom were exceedingly unsuitable.

She was however also concerned with her country.

It was her consuming ambition to make Sweden a modern Greece, a centre of the Sciences and Arts.

The ordinary people of Sweden did not care deeply about the private activities that went on in the Palace.

But they were disgusted at Christina's behaviour when she attended Church Services.

Sometimes she ostentatiously read a book during the sermon and, if she did not read, she yawned and shifted restlessly on her chair.

Once she brought her dogs with her and romped with them during the actual Service.

In her mind all was well just beyond the horizon if only she could reach it.

Lonely, Christina felt a gnawing hunger for Divine help for the future, and for absolution for the past.

She was beginning to realise that she was behaving badly.

For some time Christina had devoted her attention to entertainments and amusements to titillate her emotions.

Dances, revels and masquerades became an almost nightly occurrence.

Because they were also held on Sundays many Swedish aristocrats excused themselves from being in attendance in view of the infringements of the Holy Writ.

Christina had a passion for fancy dress, which gave her an excuse to appear as a boy or, by contrast, in the exotic dress of a Moorish concubine.

Such disguises pleased her because she could order them to be French, Classical Greek, or Castilian.

Often these entertainments would degenerate into practical joking and horse-play which had little connection with the theme she had ordered for the occasion, and at these times Christina would be the life of the party.

Late one evening in March 1652 two men cloaked and wearing large black hats disembarked from a small merchant vessel which had put into Stockholm.

In the succeeding days the two Italian gentlemen were

constantly at the Palace, ostensibly giving the Queen advice on binding one of her books, the latest trends in Western European architecture, and on the hanging of her paintings.

But the interviews were in fact concerned entirely with spiritual matters.

The two men had come to ascertain whether or not the Queen was a fit person to be received into the Catholic Church.

Their orders from the Pope were to question her closely on her religious views.

But there came the day when the unpredictable Christina abandoned all her arguments and said with an hysterical giggle:

"You would not think I was very close to becoming a Catholic, would you?"

The men did not answer, being amazed at this abrupt change on a morning when she had been particularly critical about everything they told her.

Eventually one of the two men murmured:

"Your words make us feel like men raised from the dead, Your Majesty."

Christina instantly found new objections.

"I suppose the Pope would permit me to take Communion by the Lutheran rites?" she demanded. "Say once a year — to please my people?"

The Italian shook his head.

"It would be utterly impossible."

Christina walked across to the window and looked out at the great bulk of the parish church of Stockholm where she had so often worshipped in company with her people.

Without turning round, and so quietly that her guests hardly heard her, she said:

"Then there is no help for it. I must give up my throne."

The two men left the room knowing that their mission had ended in triumph.

They remained at the Inn a few days more, hoping for a further summons, but none came.

Instead Christina sent the little page-boy with some letters. They included one to the Pope and another to Cardinal Chigi.

With these letters the two men departed from Stockholm as stealthily as they had come.

On the same day that they cast off from the quayside another vessel was putting out to sea.

In it was a Royal Courier carrying a long and rumbling letter from Christina to Prince Frederick of Hesse, trying to persuade him of the wickedness of taking the step of changing his religion, precisely as she was doing.

She then sent for her cousin Charles Gustavus and told him:

"You had better start interesting yourself in State affairs, for it will not be long before you will have to deal with deal. I have now definitely made up my mind to abdicate."

Her cousin started and said irritably:

"I cannot believe that you really intend to take this step! Frankly, Christina, I have become so accustomed to your emotional outbursts that I very rarely believe what you say!"

Christina looked at him surprised and angry before she said:

"You may not believe me at the moment, but in a few days time I shall certainly be able to convince you. You will see down at the quayside at Goteborg the crates in which I am sending out of the country all my books and manuscripts and my personal possessions."

Charles Gustavus laughed.

"If you are doing that," he said, "you may be able to abdicate, but you certainly will not be able to leave Sweden. The people of Goteborg will realise what those crates mean and the Government will forbid you to leave the country."

"You are wrong," Christina replied, "I have already told many people in the Palace that I intend to take a long holiday in Pomerania and they have accepted such an idea as reasonable. They believe that I am going there so that

I can think about the problem of succession without being worried by the day-to-day affairs of State.''

Charles shrugged his shoulders.

Even though he had not received permission to leave, he walked to the door and without bowing, left her to herself.

Nearly a year passed before she called a full meeting of the Diet at which she proposed to make an important announcement.

The old Chancellor, suspecting what the annnouncement would be told her that before he could summon the Diet, the nature of the announcement would have to be discussed with the Senate.

Christina brusquely informed them that she proposed to announce her resignation as Queen, and to obtain the formal permission of the Diet.

The Members of the Senate were dumbfounded that she did not ask their advice even as to what form her announcement should take.

A few of them begged her to alter her mind.

The meeting degenerated into an argument which Christina settled by striding out of the room.

Queen Christina's decision to abdicate created a world-wide sensation.

On June 6th the final scene was enacted.

Once again in the lofty old hall of the Castle Christina entered in full regalia, followed immediately by the King Elect.

While the Act of Abdication was read and put in front of her to sign, the Crown's Officers of the Realm placed the crown on her head and gave her the sceptre and golden orb to hold.

The Sword of State and the Keys of the Kingdom lay on cushions beside her.

The moment came when the Queen died and a King was born.

The ceremonial had been carefully rehearsed, but at the

last moment Count Brahe refused to walk forward and remove the crown from her head.

Christina gave him a look of hatred and removed it herself.

She stood up and took off the Royal cloak of purple.

It was immediately seized by a score of Members of the Diet, who rushed forward and grabbed it.

Christina stood like a statue while they quarrelled over it and ripped it to pieces to obtain a souvenir.

Above the hubbub, wearing a dress of plain white silk, she made her speech of farewell.

After again repeating that she had tried to do her best for her country and asserting that she had done nothing for which she could reproach herself, she made a brief and cold speech about the qualities of the new King.

When it was all over Christina spent the rest of the day prostrate on her bed.

The old nervous exhaustion, which made her body almost rigid had returned.

Dimly she heard the bells of the old Cathedral ringing and soon there came the crash of cannon firing a salute.

The Coronation of Charles Gustavus was taking place — the reign of Queen Christina had come to an end.

On the evening of the day that Christina abdicated a State Banquet had been arranged and the new King sent a personal request that she should attend.

She let her valet know that she did not wish to wear any special dress for the occasion, then ordered him to fetch a pair of scissors.

When he returned with them, she commanded him to cut her hair short as a boy's.

The valet was dumbfounded because Christina's tresses were the most attractive part of her appearance.

"Cut them off," she ordered, "I have given away my Kingdom; I certainly do not mind losing my natural crown."

The effect of her shorn head was all that she could desire.

She arrived late at the Banqueting Hall where everyone was already standing beside the tables, not daring to sit down until the King gave the order, and this he had no intention of doing until Christina was present.

A buzz of excitement ran among the guests when they saw her at the door, and she smiled at them disdainfully.

The King went over to her and escorted her to her seat.

The Banquet then began, but Christina was something of a skeleton at the feast for everyone was embarrassed and even the King could not persuade her into conversation.

"I have ordered," the King said to her, "twelve of our best warships to be ready for instant sailing tomorrow. My Captains have orders to show you every deference as a member of the Royal House of Vasa."

Christina nodded with satisfaction.

She then asked a series of questions about the transport of her books and art treasures.

Having satisfied her on these points, she arose and left the Banquet without a word of apology or farewell.

It was a wet and stormy night and as soon as she reached her own apartments, she scribbled a message which she handed to a servant, commanding him to give it to the King.

In it she explained that because of the weather she had decided that she would not want the battleships after all.

She then called for her Secretary and asked him to bring her some pistols, a carbine and the shabbiest men's clothes he could find.

Within an hour she was on her way from Upsala riding on horseback and escorted by only five gentlemen.

They were headed by Steinberg, who had been promoted to the rank of Count and held the position of Master of the Queen's Horse although in practice he was Christina's Secretary.

She reached Stockholm long after midnight and spent the following day writing letters to various friends abroad.

Then she went on to pay a visit to her mother, but the

Queen Mother, ageing and ill, had nothing to say.

In December she announced that her preparations for her journey to Brussels were complete.

She travelled by water in a barge which was decorated above the water-line with gold, and armed with twelve pieces of cannon. A dozen horses drew the barge in relays.

She approached Brussels late in the afternoon, as darkness was falling.

By the time she had disembarked it was past midnight, but the streets were still crammed with curious onlookers.

Despite the slush and snow which had fallen earlier, carpets had been laid along the streets which led to the Archduke's Palace.

Christina walked along them bowing with delight at her reception and pausing so often so that she could be admired that it was past two o'clock in the morning when she greeted the Archduke.

She was so excited that she refused to go to bed and walked restlessly about the Palace to find windows from which she could see the still illuminated City.

She complained petulantly when at dawn, the torches disappeared and the bonfires died down.

Later that day, in the private Chapel of the Palace, she made her secret profession of the Catholic faith.

It was, according to her, a secret one, because she still had not completely organised her financial matters with Sweden.

But the secrecy was somewhat nullified because she arranged for cannon fire at the precise moment when she was given absolution.

Christina had created all the notoriety she could possibly desire, yet she felt desperately rootless.

Her conversion was ostensibly a private matter, and Rome ordered the delay of any public celebrations until she made a more formal profession of faith.

She was thus officially neither Lutheran nor Catholic, and probably never in her life did she so vehemently desire to identify herself with some religion.

When the news reached Stockholm that Christina was planning to make a public statement of her conversion, the new King was deeply worried, not only because of the political repercussions that might occur, but because he feared that the Estates, urged on by the Clergy, would deprive her of her revenues.

He decided to appeal to her either to return to Sweden, or to abandon her plans, by sending as an emissary a young man whom he knew she particularly liked.

This was Count Tott who had an audience with Christina and stated the King's views.

Christina however was quite unimpressed and he then told her with brutal frankness of the general feeling in Sweden.

He stressed that she was in very real danger of being reduced to complete poverty.

Christina angrily refused to change her mind.

"I gave up the throne so that I could have freedom," she told him. "The Swedish people forget that they did not give me the crown; I inherited it as a Vasa. Just as I had a right to it by birth, I have also a right to renounce it should I so desire."

Christina arrived in Rome on December 19th, and on being introduced to the Pope, she threw herself prone on the ground and kissed his toe.

He took her by the hand and escorted her to a throne covered in crimson velvet and had a brief talk with her, being careful to keep all doors wide open.

On December 23rd, 1655, she was told that everything was ready, and she left the town secretly and went to an Inn where she changed into a costume which she had designed as being typical of an Amazon.

She then rode at the head of a procession through lines of troops and great crowds to the Square in front of St. Peter's.

The Priests conducted her to the Pope's Chapel where

she was confirmed, taking the name of Alexandra as a compliment to the Pope himself and to the great warrior King whom she admired and considered herself to be remarkably like, both in character and ability.

On that day Christina behaved as well as the Papal authorities could desire, but the excitement of the subsequent celebrations soon banished her propriety.

When she attended Mass, she often giggled and talked even through the most solemn parts of the Service.

The Pope, hearing of this sent her a rosary with an exhortation that she should use it while she attended Mass to keep her mind off worldly things.

Christina took the rosary, examined its worth, and then threw it on a table.

"I did not become a Catholic to tell beads," she told the horrified emissary.

Christina's inevitable reaction to her new mode of life was not long delayed.

She tried to escape from a growing sense of unhappiness by filling every hour of the day and night with activity.

Sensitive to the fact that she was no longer a reigning Queen, she attempted to create notoriety for herself by gaucherie and contemptuous manners.

Every woman who was not of Royal blood was forbidden to sit in her presence, and Christina deliberately kept them on their feet until some of the less robust ladies, weighed down by their heavy costumes, fainted from fatigue.

Male guests, by contrast were treated as equals whatever their lineage or background.

The Pope, worried by the behaviour of Christina's suite appointed a new and brilliant Cardinal Dezio Azzolini, to bring some sort of order to Christina's household.

He was an aristocrat who had adopted an ecclesiastical career at an early age and his rise had been meteoric.

By the time he was thirty-one he was a Cardinal, and he had been the strong influence in the election of

Alexander as Pope less than a year before.

Extremely handsome, with a delicately curved mouth, long sensitive fingers, and a subtle, dexterous wit, Dezio Assolini would have attracted many women, let alone the susceptible Christina.

As soon as the Cardinal arrived and put a stop to the most blatant excesses of Christina's retinue the outwitted rogues not unnaturally began a campaign of slander.

The Pope took no notice of it beyond asking — and receiving — Azzolini's assurance that his relationship with Christina as merely official and entirely innocent.

For a time the rumours died down.

Then, during Christina's convalescence they began again — and from a different source.

The tavern talk was a belated echo of the ominous stories which were reported to the Papal authorities by dignitaries of the City who were shocked rather than intrigued.

The Pope, with all the knowledge of human frailty that his high office gave him prayed that time and distance would prevent this exasperating young woman from destroying the reputation and career of one of the most capable men in the Vatican.

He was told by a most reliable source that the Cardinal, dressed as a wandering troubadour could be seen any night beneath Christina's bedroom window, serenading her in a cracked voice and plucking an execrable tune from a lyre.

He was also informed of the scandalous jingle which was being repeated all over Rome, which went:

"Now her dear Azzolini in Rome
So charmed her with delight
From him she could not live a day
Nor pass a tedious night."

The Pope decided that Christina's departure from Rome should be treated with great urgency.

Cardinal Azzolini was not in attendance when Christina stepped aboard the Papal galley at Civita Vecchia.

But it was seen that she was clasping a locket on a chain

to her bosom as she paid her respects to the aged Cardinals who had been chosen to bid her godspeed.

Inside was a miniature of Azzolini.

As the vessel moved out to sea she kept to her curtained cabin, and no one accompanying her could persuade her to come out and enjoy the sea air.

She was in a delightful reverie, reliving wild moments of love – and passion.

Christina's crazy eccentricities continued in various parts of Europe.

In February, 1689 she was stricken with malaria and during the illness erysipelas broke out.

For some days she hovered between life and death, but to everyone's surprise she slowly recovered.

In April, she fell ill again and angered and upset at the attempted rape of one of her maids she flew into a rage.

She died shortly afterwards on April 19th, 1689.

Azzolini was heartbroken at the ex-Queen's death, and he only survived her for two months.

QUEEN CHRISTINA OF SWEDEN

H.M. KING CAROL OF ROUMANIA
1893 – 1953

Prince Carol of Roumania was the son of King Ferdinand I and Princess Marie of Great Britain.

He began to give his father and mother a lot of anxiety and trouble before he even grew out of his teens.

His mother's cousin King George V of Great Britain would have described him as a 'cad' and he would have been right.

Carol was a womanizer and so weak willed that almost any woman could influence him.

He became infatuated with 'Zizi' Lambrino a Roumanian girl from a good family, and eloped with her to Odessa, where he persuaded the Orthodox Clergy to marry them in the Cathedral in August 1918.

When the news reached Bucharest, the King and Queen were furious with their son and demanded the immediate annulment of the marriage, which took place in January 1919.

Carol continued to live with 'Zizi', and in January 1920 she gave birth to a son in Bucharest.

The child was not acknowledged by the King and Queen and they arranged for Carol to marry Princess Helen of Greece.

The marriage took place at Athens in March 1921, but despite the fact that the Princess was beautiful and accomplished, Carol never loved her and soon left her after she had given birth prematurely to a son.

His taste ran to more brassy and obvious women and in 1925 he caused another scandal by eloping with the half-Jewish, red-haired divorcee Elena (known as Magda) Lupescu.

Carol renounced his rights to the throne and the King and Queen accepted it with great relief.

King Ferdinand died two years later in July 1927, and was succeeded by his six-year-old grandson Michael, the son of Carol and Princess Helen, whose marriage was dissolved the following year.

Michael reigned under a three-man Council of Regency headed by his uncle Prince Nicholas until in June 1930, his father returned to Roumania at the Invitation of the Prime Minister.

He was then proclaimed King Carol II, and his son Michael was demoted from King to Crown Prince.

King Carol was still completely under the influence of Magda Lupescu and behaved in a very cavalier fashion towards his mother and other members of the Royal Family.

However, he did restore the country to prosperity and proved himself a patron of the Arts, rebuilding the Royal Palace in a somewhat flamboyant style.

By 1940 he had become an absolute Monarch but on the 6th September of that year at Hitler's instigation he was forced to abdicate in favour of his son Michael.

Carol became a Royal wanderer, always accompanied by Magda Lupescu.

In June 1947 they were in Rio de Janeiro, when she fell ill, allegedly with pernicious anaemia, and was reported to be on her deathbed.

A tearful Carol married her in a moving bedside ceremony. The next day she began miraculously to recover and was soon fit and well.

Carol decided that she should become the Princess of Hohenzollern with the title of Royal Highness and got his kinsman the Prince of Hohenzollern to agree to this.

The couple eventually settled in the Portuguese resort of Estoril, a favourite haven for Royal Exiles.

Carol died at their villa there in April 1953. Magda lived until June 1977.

Her coffin lies beside Carol's in the burial Chapel of his Braganca ancestors, awaiting the day when they can be returned to Roumania.

H.M. KING CAROL OF ROUMANIA

ACKNOWLEDGEMENTS

Barbara Cartland wishes to thank the following people very much:

Montgomery Hyde, "The Empress Catherine and Prince Dashkov"; Aubrey Richardson, "The Lover of Queen Elizabeth"; Gina Kaus, "Catherine The Great"; Stafan Zweig, "The Queen of Scots"; Eva Scott, "Six Stuart Sovereigns 1512-1701"; Lt.-Col. Andrew C. P. Haggard, "Sidelights on the Court of France"; Count D'Ornano, "Life and Loves of Marie Walewska"; Barbara Cartland, "Book of Beauty and Health"; Sir Herbert Maxwell, "Sixty Years a Queen"; H. K. Prescot, "The Early and Middle Ages"; Edmund d'Auvergne, "A Queen at Bay"; Martin Hume, "The Wives of Henry VIII"; "The Illustrated London News 1900 and 1902"; Neville Connell, "Anne"; Octave Aubry, "Eugenie Empress of France"; Baring Gould, "The Tragedy of The Caesars"; P. W. Sergeant, "The Empress Josephine"; Barbara Cartland, "The Outrageous Queen"; Stenton, "William The Conqueror"; Curties, "A Forgotten Prince of Wales"; Fletcher and Kipling, "A History of England"; Choiseul Gouffier, "Alexander I and Court of Russia"; Charles Petrie, "Louis XIV"; Dunn Paterson, "The Black Prince Edward"; Waliszewski, "Ivan The Terrible"; Cornelius Gurhitt, "August de Starke"; Maura Camazo, "Carlos II Su Corte"; Benjamin Ide Wheeler, "Alexander The Great"; G. F. Kunz, "The Book of The Pearl"; Princess Catherine Radziwill, "Sovereigns & Statesmen of Europe"; Lt.-Col. Andrew Haggard, "The Real Louis XV"; Rachel Challice, "Secret History of The Court of Spain"; Michael Senior, "Richard II"; Francoise de Bernardy, "The Princes of Monaco"; C. C. Trench, "The Royal Malady"; Harmsworth Encyclopaedia, Vol. VI; M. W. Freer, "Henry III of France and Poland"; Alfred E. T. Watson, "King Edward VII as a Sportsman"; Barbara Cartland,

"The Fragrant Flower"; Hugh Stokes, "A Prince of Pleasure Philip of France and His Court"; Michael Prawdin, "The Mad Queen of Spain"; Mrs. Bearne, "A Sister of Marie Antoinette"; Graham, "Life of Alexander II"; Jerome Dreifuss, "The Romances of Catherine and Potemkin"; Francis Cribble, "The Royal House of Portugal"; H.R.H. Prince Tomislav of Yugoslavia; Dr. Rappoport, "Leopold II King of The Belgians"; A. Hilliard Atteridge, "Napoleon's Brothers"; Wilson, "Napoleon The Man"; Frederick de Reichenberg, "Prince Metternich in Love and War"; Barbara Cartland, "The Passionate Diplomat"; Barbara Cartland, "Romantic Royal Marriages"; Edward Legge, "King Edward in His True Colours"; Barbara Cartland, "Diane de Poittiers"; "The Coronation of Their Majesties King George VI and Queen Elizabeth"; "King Albert's Book"; Sigmund Munz, "King Edward VII at Marienbad"; Walter Jerrold, "Henry VIII and His Wives"; Iain Moncreiffe and Don Pottinger, "Simple Heraldry"; Prince Michael of Greece, "Crown Jewels of Britain and Europe"; Guido Gregorietti, "Jewellery Through The Ages"; S. Baring Gould, M.A., "Farouk of Egypt"; David Randall, "Royal Follies"; Daniel George, "A Book of Characters"; Jean Plaidy, "The Spanish Inquisition"; Joanna Richardson, "La Vie Parisienne"; Anita Leslie, "Edwardians in Love"; Barbara Cartland, "The Outrageous Queen"; Barbara Cartland, "Empress of Austria"; Barbara Cartland, "A Year of Royal Days"; Virginia Cowles, "The Romanovs"; Lesley Blanch, "Wilder Shores of Love"; Barbara Cartland, "Love and Lovers"; Barbara Cartland, "Written With Love"; Nina Epton, "Lovers and the French"; Nina Epton, "Lovers and the English"; E. Barrington, "The Laughing Queen"; Beatrice Clay, "Stories of Arthur and The Round Table"; Joanna Richardson, "The Courtesans"; Nancy Mitford, "The Sun King"; G. F. Kunz, "Curious Law of Precious Stones"; G. F. Kunz, "Magic of Jewels and Charms"; William Jones, "Finger

Ring Lore"; Thomas Secombe, "Twelve Bad Men"; Dorothy Marshall, "Victoria"; Norah Lofts, "Anne Boleyn"; Arthur Vincent, "Twelve Bad Women"; E. F. Benson, "The Kaiser and English Relations"; Longworth, "The Three Empresses"; Erskin, "29 Years of Alfonso XIII of Spain"; Segur, "Marie Antoinette"; Haslip, "Marie Antoinette"; Asprey, "Frederick The Great"; Michael Prestwick, "Edward I"; John Gillingham, "Life and Times of Richard I"; Michael Senior, "Life and Times of Richard II"; Rossabi Khubilia Khan, "Khubilia Khan"; W. B. Henderson, "Life of The Emperor Nero"; Wiegall, "Nero"; R. Davey, "Sultan and His Subjects"; Cronholm, "History of Sweden"; J. S. Orvis, "A Brief History of Poland"; Joan Evans, "Magical Jewels of the Middle Ages and the Renaissance"; Antonia Fraser, "The Kings and Queens of England"; Leslie Field, "The Queens Jewels"; Maurice Ashley, "The Life and Times of King John"; Princess Michael of Kent, "Crowned in a Far Country"; Nancy Mitford, "Frederick The Great"; Suzy Jerkes, "The Royal Jewels"; Alexander von Solodkoff, "Masterpieces from The House of Fabergé"; John Lord, "The Maharajas"; Lesley Blanch, "Pavilions of The Heart"; Theo Lang, "My Darling Daisy"; Cecil Woodham Smith, "Queen Victoria"; Elizabeth Longford, "Victoria I"; Antonia Fraser, "Mary Queen of Scots"; Debretts Kings and Queens of Europe; David Williamson, Webb & Bower (Michael Joseph).

OTHER TITLES CURRENTLY AVAILABLE IN

The Royal Series

ROYAL LOVERS

ROYAL JEWELS

~

Look out for more titles
in this exciting new series in your
bookshop soon